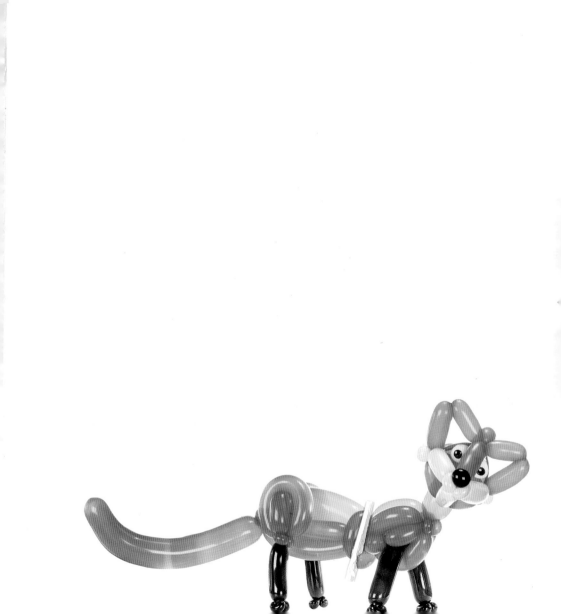

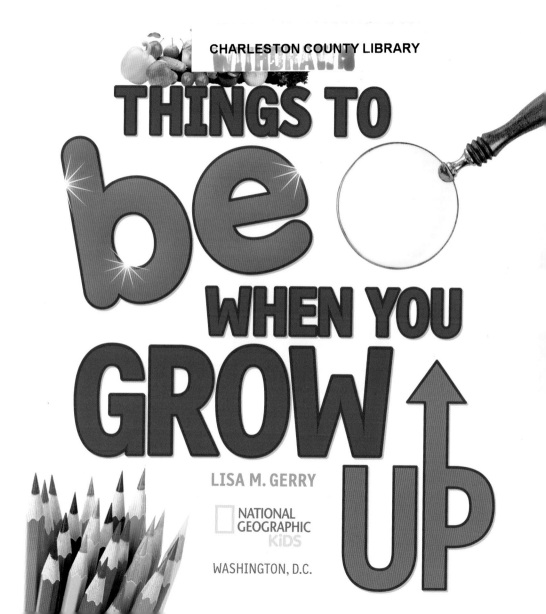

THINGS TO be WHEN YOU GROW UP

LISA M. GERRY

NATIONAL
GEOGRAPHIC
KiDS

WASHINGTON, D.C.

When I was a child, I was knocked over by a wave, and the ocean got my attention. But soon after, it was the stuff *in* the ocean that captured my imagination: **The shimmering squid, scuttling crabs, mysterious kelp forests, and vibrant coral reefs.** I've been swimming and diving ever since. As a **National Geographic explorer-in-residence,** I've made it my mission to help protect our world's oceans for future generations, like you!

I am often asked, **How do you get to be an explorer?** My answer is simple. I started out like most kids, always wondering, always curious about the world, and always asking questions. Explorers are just grown-ups who **look at the world with curiosity and wonder and seek out answers.**

In that regard, **all passionate people are explorers,** whether you're writing music lyrics and exploring new ways to mix words and sound, delving deep into the forest to uncover rare mushrooms, or tracking iceberg movement across the Arctic.

The world is full of possibilities, mysteries, and opportunities. It's your job to start thinking about **what interests you.** It might be one thing that hits you early on (quite literally in my case), or many different things. And that's OK! You'll find out that **many cool careers combine disciplines and passions.**

Whether you love cooking, listening to music, writing, taking photographs, climbing, watching movies, all of those things, or something else, hopefully this book will **get your creative mind fired up** and offer some cool inspiration! And don't be afraid to dive in, dig deep, and **get a little muddy along your path to discovery.**

So go ahead—flip through and **have fun!**

DR. SYLVIA EARLE
OCEANOGRAPHER AND NATIONAL GEOGRAPHIC EXPLORER-IN-RESIDENCE

The world is full of possibilities, mysteries, and opportunities. It's your job to start thinking about what interests you.

ICE-CREAM FLAVOR DEVELOPER

6

KIRSTEN, "FLAVOR GURU"

1

Making ice cream, hands down, has to be one of the coolest jobs ever. And not just because it's actually cold.
It's because you get to make ice cream. As your job.

Meet Kirsten Schimoler. She's a "flavor guru" at Ben & Jerry's. "I am always searching for new flavors," says Schimoler. "I get inspiration from magazines, blogs, restaurants, childhood memories, and even suggestions from customers."

HERE SCHIMOLER GIVES US THE INSIDE SCOOP ON HER DELICIOUS DREAM JOB.

Q When did you know you wanted to make ice cream your career?

A I've always loved ice cream—one of my earliest favorites was mint chocolate chip. Then I moved to Waterbury, Vermont [U.S.A.], when I was a kid, and one of our first stops was the Ben & Jerry's factory. We took a tour and sampled some ice cream. Learning about ice cream that day was part of what inspired me to study **food science.**

Q What was your path to becoming a flavor guru at Ben & Jerry's?

A My family has always been involved in the food industry, so food and flavors became a passion for me at an early age. I went to Cornell University, where I studied food science. About a year and a half after I graduated, I got my first role as a flavor guru at Ben & Jerry's. During my career, I have done a lot of on-the-job-training and technical training specific to the science of ice cream and frozen desserts.

> **FOOD SCIENCE = THE STUDY OF THE PHYSICAL, CHEMICAL, AND BIOCHEMICAL PROPERTIES OF FOOD.**

Q What's a typical day like for you?

A There is no real typical one for me, but my days often include visiting the factory, working in the lab/kitchen, working on my computer, going to meetings, talking to consumers, tasting samples, and laughing. You always need to laugh!

Q Do you eat ice cream most days?

A Most days, I eat a little bit of ice cream. But because I eat ice cream often, I eat very small servings. Just a taste, with a small spoon!

Q Is there anything that might surprise people about your job?

A There is a lot more to it than just eating! I use chemistry, microbiology, math, and problem-solving to do what I do. Sometimes I am in the factory until

4 a.m., because we're making a new flavor, and I need to make sure it looks great. Also, my job can get messy—I often am covered in ice cream!

Q What are some of the flavors you've developed? Any favorites?

A At this point, I have worked on more than 20 flavors. I developed the whole Greek Frozen Yogurt line, and, most recently, the Vegan Almond Milk line. Two of my favorite ice creams that I developed have been Chocolate Peppermint Crunch—an ode to Thin Mint cookies—and **Candy Bar Pie.**

Q Do you have a favorite ingredient to work with?

A I don't have one specific ingredient I like to use, but I like to develop flavors so that you can get a little bit of each component in every bite. That creates a specific taste, which makes the flavor feel like a complete dessert.

CANDY BAR PIE = PEANUT BUTTER ICE CREAM WITH FUDGE FLAKES, CHOCOLATE NOUGAT, AND SWEET AND SALTY PRETZEL SWIRLS. *UM, YUM!*

Q Are there any ingredients you'd like to incorporate into a flavor but haven't yet?

A Living in Vermont, I love maple syrup. I'd love to be able to make an amazing maple flavor.

2

MUSHROOM

If you've ever gone on an Easter egg or scavenger hunt, you know what a thrill it can be to look for and find a tiny hidden treasure. That's what mushroom foragers do every day—it's like a Where's Waldo of the woods. They travel across the country, spend all day hiking in remote locations, and sometimes even camp in forests overnight in search of delicious and in-demand fungi. Then they pluck the mushrooms out of the ground, or cut them with scissors or a knife, haul them home, and sell them for a pretty penny to restaurants and chefs.

Five Fun Facts About Mushrooms

1 The Alba white mushroom, from the Alba region in Italy, sells for $2,000 per pound (0.45 kg). Yowza! That's a fancy fungus!

2 In France and Italy, mushroom hunters train dogs to sniff out mushrooms. Sometimes, they train pigs, although the pigs have been known to eat the mushrooms before the humans can get to them.

FORAGER

inspiration station

Right now, you are in the brainstorming phase of choosing a career. The sky is the limit. Anything is possible. The bigger your dreams, the better! What are you curious about? What interests you? Your job right now is to explore the subjects that you find fascinating and do the things that make you happy.

3 One portabella mushroom has more potassium than a banana.

4 Mushrooms are made up of about 90 percent water.

5 Mushrooms aren't classified as either plants or animals. They have their own kingdom classification: Fungi.

3

Beekeeper

A **beekeeper** is someone who maintains hives of honeybees and harvests what the bees produce, including honey and beeswax.

MEET LEIGH-KATHRYN BONNER.
She is a fourth generation beekeeper who works with companies such as Burt's Bees. Her great-grandfather was a beekeeper, and her grandfather and uncle still keep bees. Growing up, she'd visit her grandfather and uncle's farm in Farmville, North Carolina, U.S.A., and watch as they dipped their bare hands into the buzzing swarms of honeybees.

While some folks might be terrified, Bonner was fascinated.

Then, as a college freshman at North Carolina State University, she took a science class called Bees and Beekeeping. "I fell in love with beekeeping even more," says Bonner. "And I loved that I got to spend time with my uncle and grandfather learning about something that is so important to our family."

Here Bonner explains what all the BUZZ about BEES is about …

What's the trick to not getting stung?

If I wear my suit, I don't get stung at all. But, hardheadedness runs in my family, and because my grandpa and uncle don't ever wear suits, I don't want to wear them either. The thing is, my grandpa and uncle don't swell up like I do when they get stung, so I really should be better about wearing my suit! We also use a smoker when working in the hives, which calms the bees.

SMOKER = A HAND-HELD CANISTER, USUALLY MADE FROM TIN OR STEEL, THAT IS USED TO BURN FUEL AND THEN EMIT SMOKE FROM A SPOUT AT THE TOP.

What's something people might not know about bees?

Most people who tell you they have been stung by a honeybee were actually stung by a yellow jacket. Honeybees are extremely calm. And they're the only bee or wasp that will die if they sting you, so they avoid stinging at all costs.

What's your favorite part about being a beekeeper?

I love that every time you open up a hive, there is something new to learn and see. My favorite part though, hands down, is giving someone who has never seen bees before a hands-on lesson at our hives. There's an incredible excitement and curiosity from people the first time they see bees up close. It's the most rewarding thing about beekeeping.

You started a company called Bee Downtown—can you talk a bit about that?

I started the company when I was a junior in college. After I graduated, I decided to keep building the company, and now it's my full-time job. I put beehives on rooftops in cities to help companies get attention and interest from the public and potential customers. Beekeeping is not just for rural areas—in the last 10 years, there has been a surge of urban beekeeping in cities around the world.

What are some of your favorite uses for honey?

I love to bake with honey. Honey is a natural sweetener, and it tastes so good in cookies and cakes. I also like to drizzle it over vanilla ice cream.

Also, many people don't know this, but honey is one of the best things you can put on a burn wound. Honey is antibacterial and has wonderful healing properties. So, next time you burn your hand pulling cookies out of the oven, try putting honey on the burn instead of Neosporin.

FUN FACT!

80% OF THE WORLD'S FOOD is pollinated by honeybees.

What are some of the necessary skills or traits of someone who would like to be a beekeeper?

Anyone who wants to be a beekeeper can be a beekeeper. As long as you have a yard or rooftop, you can have bees! A good beekeeper is patient, loves animals, and is caring. Just like with any pet, you have to remember to take care of them so that they stay healthy. If you take good care of your bees, not only will you learn a lot, you will get lots of delicious honey to eat, too.

Why are bees so important?

In recent years, in the United States alone, we have lost more than a third of our bee population. Honeybees are our most important pollinator—in fact, 80 percent of the world's food is pollinated by honeybees—so, it's crucial that we protect and take care of them as best we can.

Lyricist

If you've ever had a song stuck in your head, you know the power of catchy lyrics. Lyricists are the magicians who string words together to make megahit songs. With musical talent and a way with words, you could write songs for advertising jingles, musicals, or even pop stars.

WAIT, I DIDN'T KNOW *THEY WROTE THAT!*

Check out these musicians and the hit songs they wrote for other artists.

1 Jessie J wrote the Miley Cyrus hit "Party in the USA."

2 Harry Styles wrote Ariana Grande's song "Just a Little Bit of Your Heart."

3 The Dream and Christina Milian wrote Justin Bieber's "Baby."

4 Sia wrote "Pretty Hurts" for Beyonce.

5 Dolly Parton wrote "I Will Always Love You," a song made famous by Whitney Houston.

Golf Ball
DIVER

Forget **coral reefs** and beautiful schools of **rainbow-colored fish**—these scuba divers strap on their tanks to swim in dirty, sometimes **alligator-infested** lakes on golf courses. But why, you might ask? To collect the **hundreds of balls** that were mistakenly hit there by golfers, which they wash and resell. It's a **treasure hunter's dream** ... if you don't mind the leeches, water snakes, and **snapping turtles**.

6

TV WRITER

Next time you flip on the tube to watch your **favorite show,** pay attention to the story and what your favorite characters are saying. Almost all of it—from the **dialogue** to the **action**—was created by a **television writer.** Together, a **team** of writers decide what should happen in every episode, and then they **write the script.**

Check out this page from a script for the National Geographic digital series *You Wanna Be A What!?*, which features scientists with awesome jobs.

YOU WANNA BE A WHAT?!
Kakani Katija—Jellyfish Whisperer

TEXT:
Jellyfish Whisperer

NARRATOR:
Kakani Katija follows jellyfish all over the world.

NARRATOR:
In Palau, she dives in the famous jellyfish lake, where millions of golden jellies move through the water every day.

POPUP:
Golden jellyfish get their color from the golden algae living inside them.

POPUP:
The jellies follow the path of the sun as they move across the lake from east to west.

NARRATOR:
In Panama, Kakani braves venomous sea snakes and inky waters on open-ocean night dives.

NARRATOR:
She's searching for long strings of jelly-like salps.

POPUP:
Salps use jet propulsion to move—they pump water right through their gelatinous bodies.

NARRATOR:
Kakani uses fluorescent dyes to see the way water gets pushed around the creatures as they move.

NARRATOR:
It works for humans, too ...

POPUP:
Kakani was a competitive ice dancer before she traded in her skates for scuba gear.

NARRATOR:
Kakani also uses lasers to measure the jellies' progress through the water.

POPUP:
The lasers light the animals up without injuring them.

NARRATOR:
Why does Kakani do all this? To figure out how the movement of animals mixes the water in the ocean.

NARRATOR:
Kakani believes they may be as important to a healthy ocean—and even the climate of Earth—as the wind and the tides.

POPUP:
Jellyfish don't have bones, hearts, or brains. They rely on their nervous system to move.

NARRATOR:
So, who is Kakani Katija?

NARRATOR:
She's a laser-shooting, dye-squirting, scuba-diving, jellyfish-wrangling ...

NARRATOR:
... BIOENGINEER!

7

NATURAL HISTORY PHOTOGRAPHER

Would you be up for braving a swarm of honeybees in California or getting up close and personal with a giant beetle in Brazil? Would you like to come face to tiny face with tree frogs in Panama or get to hear the flutter of hummingbird wings in the Bahamas?

MEET **ANAND VARMA**, NATIONAL GEOGRAPHIC EXPLORER AND NATURAL HISTORY PHOTOGRAPHER. FOR HIM, THESE ADVENTURES ARE ALL IN A DAY'S WORK.

HOW DID YOU BECOME INTERESTED IN PHOTOGRAPHY?

At the end of high school, I found my dad's old camera and decided to take it with me on hiking and camping trips. It was a fun way to document the places I went and the creatures I found. I didn't take it seriously, though, until I landed a job as a photographic assistant halfway through my time in college. I worked for a photographer who focused on natural history stories, and I saw that I could use a camera as a tool to explore the world and share my discoveries.

WHAT DID YOU STUDY IN SCHOOL? DOES IT HELP WITH YOUR WORK NOW?

I studied biology in college, and it is central to the work that I do now. Photography is merely my excuse for wandering around the world and learning as much as I can about the natural history of our planet. My former classmates and professors in the biology department will help me find interesting subjects to photograph. Also, my background in biology helps me communicate the complicated science behind subjects in an accessible and engaging way.

HOW DO YOU CONTINUE TO STUDY AND IMPROVE YOUR CRAFT?

My goal is to make images that are surprising and engaging. To do that, I develop new photography techniques

for every story that I work on. For my first story on parasites, I learned how to use fiber optics and focusing lenses so that I could control beams of light down to the millimeter scale. Right now, I am learning how to control the timing of my camera and my lights so that I can reveal the lightning-fast movements of hummingbirds.

IS THERE AN EXPERIENCE THAT YOU'VE HAD WORKING ON AN ASSIGNMENT THAT'S BEEN MOST MEMORABLE TO YOU?

My most memorable experience was working on a story about biodiversity. I was snorkeling just offshore of an island called Mo'orea in French Polynesia. It was dark, and I floated quietly, watching for creatures to enter the beam of my flashlight. I can still remember the bizarre, alien-like life forms that appeared out of the darkness in front of me. All kinds of tiny fish, baby crabs, and polka-dotted snails floated by me that night. Then, a baby flounder

swam up to me and perched on my mask. It was almost entirely transparent, except its iridescent skeleton sparkled with rainbow colors.

WHAT DO YOU HOPE PEOPLE GET FROM VIEWING YOUR WORK?

In my photographs, I like to show creatures that are just slightly too small or actions that are a bit too fast for us to see. By revealing these details, I want to show people that there is so much beauty and wonder out there for us to explore if we just slow down and look more closely.

WHAT ARE SOME OF THE NECESSARY SKILLS OR TRAITS OF SOMEONE WHO WOULD LIKE TO BE A NATURAL HISTORY PHOTOGRAPHER?

I think the most important traits are patience, perseverance, and attention to detail. You ultimately have to figure out a way to create something unique, and that is a hard thing to do. It takes a lot of time to get good at whatever you decide to pursue, and it is a scary thing to commit to doing something that you have never done before. You have to keep going even when you think there is no hope or that you have failed. If you can stick it out long enough and learn from your mistakes, then it is possible to make an interesting and useful contribution to the world. That can be through photography, science, or any number of other fields.

WHAT ADVICE WOULD YOU GIVE TO STUDENTS JUST STARTING TO CONSIDER THEIR FUTURE CAREERS?

I think it is really important to get experience in whatever field you are interested in as soon as possible. I wanted to be a biologist for as long as I can remember, but as soon as I started getting experience in that field, I learned I didn't like it as much as I thought. I landed a job as a photographic assistant by accident, and I figured out photography was the perfect job for me. It is hard to know what each profession is like until you actually do it yourself, so I think it is really helpful to seek internships, volunteer opportunities, or other experiences that show you what it is actually like to do that job.

VOICE-OVER
ACTOR

Voice actors may **NOT BE SEEN ON SCREEN,** but their voices are heard. The best are great actors with **DISTINCTIVE, UNIQUE VOICES.**

8

FIVE COOL CAREER PATHS

1
ANIMATED TV SHOWS AND MOVIES
"Hello, I've never met a talking dog before ..."

2
AUDIO BOOKS
"And then she said, 'This is going to be great!'"

3

MOVIE TRAILERS
"Once upon a time, in a faraway land ..."

4

TV COMMERCIALS
"Side effects may include ..."

INSTRUCTIONAL VIDEOS

5

"Make sure all carry-on items are safely stowed in an overhead bin ..."

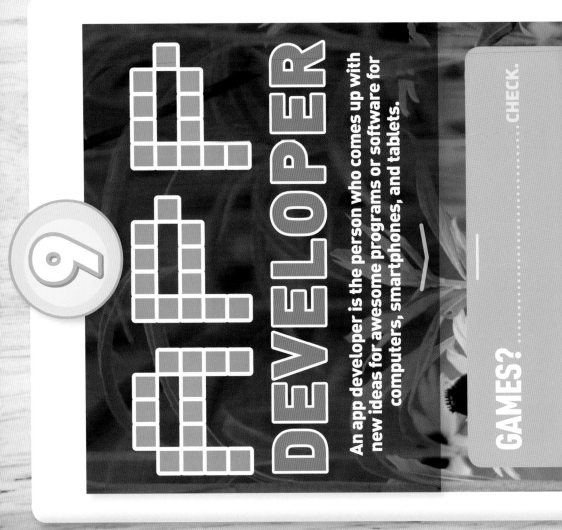

APP DEVELOPER

An app developer is the person who comes up with new ideas for awesome programs or software for computers, smartphones, and tablets.

GAMES? .... CHECK.

9

SILLY SOUND EFFECTS?.........CHECK.

PHOTOS AND VIDEO? .....CHECK, CHECK.

There's an app for
just about everything.

PROFESSIONAL

PUSHER

WiLd & wAcKy!

WHILE THERE MAY BE "NO PUSHING!" ON THE PLAYGROUND, there *is* pushing on the trains and subways in Japan—and plenty of it. Not all of it is from harried passengers, either. Transit employees called oshiya, or pushers, help smoosh passengers into already packed cars during rush hour so that the doors can close and no clothing—or limb!—gets stuck.

SPORTS TEAM PHYSICIAN

Being a sports team physician is a **cool mix** of a few different interests and areas of expertise. It combines a love of helping people, sports, **working** with **athletes,** and, of course, medicine.

These doctors sit on the sidelines with professional teams and provide care as needed. Their ultimate goal is to work with the athletes to **prevent any injuries.** But when athletes do get hurt, they diagnose, treat, and work to rehabilitate them.

GO, TEAM DOCTOR, GO!

inspiration station

Remember, you don't have to pick just one interest or area of expertise. Many jobs are a combination of different subjects. For example: Do you like music *and* the law? Consider becoming a music attorney. Do you like sports *and* writing? You could be a sports journalist! Do you like cooking *and* business? How about becoming a restaurant owner?!

12

HOLLYWOOD ANIMAL TRAINER

FOR EVERY MOVIE STARRING A MONKEY, COMMERCIAL FEATURING A CAT, AND DISNEY CHANNEL SHOW WITH A DOG IN THE CAST, THERE'S A DEDICATED TRAINER WORKING WITH THAT ANIMAL BEHIND THE SCENES. SOMEONE HAS TRAINED IT TO WALK INTO A ROOM, BARK, OR ROLL OVER ON CUE.

What's it like training Hollywood's most popular pets? Meet dog trainer extraordinaire Mathilde de Cagny.

De Cagny has trained furry, four-legged stars for many films, including *Hotel for Dogs*, *Marley and Me*, *Hugo*, and *We Bought a Zoo*. Here she talks about how she got started, some of her favorite projects, and what it is she loves about her job.

⭐ HOW DID YOU GET STARTED TRAINING ANIMALS?

I was born with a love of animals, and I was always very curious about animal psychology. After I graduated, I moved from Paris [France] to Los Angeles [U.S.A.]. One day, I saw a cat food commercial where the cat had to jump up on the table and knock down the bag in order to get to his food. I realized then that training animals was indeed a job. And, from then on, I was obsessed with it. I thought, *This*

is what I'm going to do—I'm going to train animals for motion pictures and TV! So, I watched a bunch of movies with animals, wrote down the trainers' names, and then I contacted them and volunteered for their companies. I got really lucky, because my first

dog was one that I found in a shelter—I loved his look, he was very fluffy and super cute—and he was chosen for the movies *Back to the Future 2* and *3*.

⭐ WHAT DO YOU LOOK FOR IN A DOG THAT YOU'RE GOING TO TRAIN?

Well, 80 percent of my dogs are rescues, so the goal is to pick up dogs in need and give them a second chance. For example, I trained the dog in *Anchorman 1* and *2*, and he was actually found in a parking lot in Virginia. It doesn't have to be the most beautiful dog, but there has to be something about him that's going to make me look twice—maybe some funny ears or a tongue hanging out. I like them when they're not perfect. As for their demeanor, I like dogs that are really hyper and outgoing. I like dogs that may have too much energy for a family, because there is never too much energy for the type of work that we do.

I have to be honest with you, usually when I read a script, I think,

I'll never be able to do it! But training is a process, and when you take your time and try out different approaches, ultimately, you get to where you need to go. In *Hugo*, there's a scene where the dog is in a clock tower, and he's looking for the main character. It was shot in such a way that I couldn't be anywhere close to the dog. So, I taught her how to search for treats. Then I hid radios in the clock tower, and I called her from downstairs,

through the radios. That way, I was able to get her moving around the tower. It looked great!

I want to emphasize that I train with positive reinforcement, and I always make sure it feels like a fun game for the dog. The clicker is a great tool to use, and training is a great way to bond with your dog.

I love so many things, but I love the animals more than anything. To be able to spend my days with them is such a blessing.

FIGHT

CHOREOGRAPHER

13

Every roundhouse kick, every HEAD-BUTT, and every "Hi-Yah!" is planned and practiced when it's on the stage or on screen. And just like with dance, the person who designs the sequence of movements is called a choreographer. But with this kind of choreography, there are more *Pow!*s than pliés.

Fight choreographers train actors **how to use WEAPONS** from other time periods, such as swords and bayonets. They can teach certain styles of fighting, including fencing or karate, and they show actors how to make punches and kicks look realistic without actually making contact.

A **big fight scene** is just as involved as a **high-speed CAR CHASE** or a dramatic dance number. There are very high stakes and lots of moving parts. So, in addition to being an expert fighter and knowing how to work with actors, a fight choreographer has to have a keen understanding of theater, TV, and film. **ACTION!**

KAPOW!

39

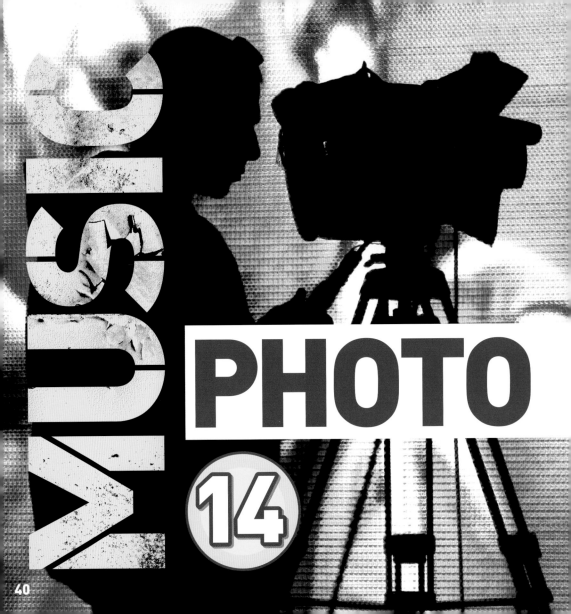

MUSIC

PHOTO

14

40

GRAPHER

Want to know how to bag the best seats at a concert? Become a music photographer. Usually, these individuals are behind special barricades, INCHES FROM THE STAGE, as musicians rock out or croon in front of them. These MUSIC-LOVING VISUAL ARTISTS are often given assignments from magazines, websites, or even the bands themselves looking for that perfect action shot. And being up close and personal helps ensure they capture every guitar solo, drumstick twirl, hair flip, and dance move.

WiLd & wAcKy!

SNAKE
milker

MOST PEOPLE DO EVERYTHING WITHIN THEIR POWER TO STAY AS FAR AWAY FROM A POISONOUS SNAKE'S FANGS AS POSSIBLE. But snake milkers aren't "most people." They handle deadly snakes, such as pit vipers and rattlesnakes, on a daily basis to help save lives. When a poisonous snake bites, it releases venom, which paralyzes or kills its prey, making it easier for the snake to eat. But the snake's venom can also be used to make antivenin, which is what saves people who have been bitten. It's also used in treatments for other medical conditions, like high blood pressure.

To collect a **snake's venom,** the snake milker holds the snake's head, pressing down in **just the right spot** to get the snake to open its mouth. Then the snake's **fangs** are pushed onto the side of a glass jar or funnel. The snake then excretes its venom, **a yellowish liquid,** which is sent off to **hospitals, pharmaceutical companies,** and **medical researchers.**

RADIO
HOST

16

SWAG

Some are serious; some are silly. Some discuss politics; others make **prank calls.** Radio personalities are as varied as the shows they host, which can cover topics ranging from **cars to classical music.** They cover the news, give updates on weather and traffic, **interview celebrities,** play music, and more. Radio hosts need to have a great voice, a **positive attitude,** and a likable personality to keep listeners tuned in.

FUN FACT!

In 1933, **PRESIDENT FRANKLIN D. ROOSEVELT** began addressing the American people in **RADIO BROADCASTS** that became known as **"FIRESIDE CHATS."** He used **SIMPLE, CASUAL LANGUAGE** to discuss and explain important political issues. Then, in 1982, **PRESIDENT RONALD REGAN** began a tradition of weekly radio addresses, which **EVERY PRESIDENT** since has continued.

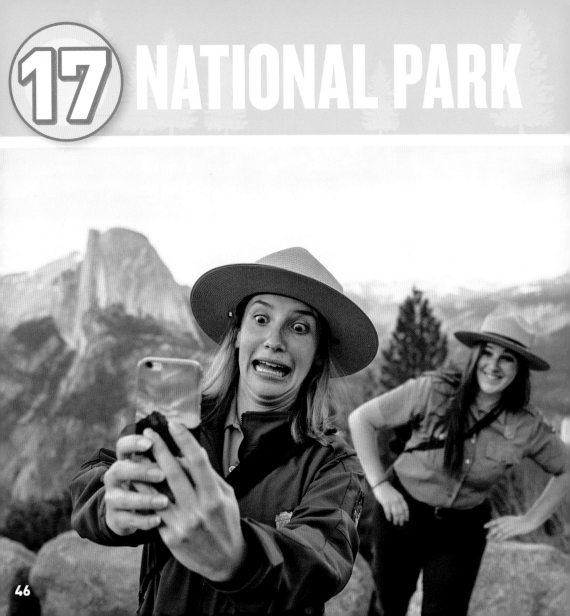

SERVICE EMPLOYEE

There are more than 400 sites in the National Park System. This includes battlefields, monuments, seashores, and even the White House! And there are about 22,000 people—from scientists and historians to electricians and police officers—who work at these awesome spots. They do all sorts of things, like study a site's plants and animals, educate visitors about the significance of a historic location, provide first aid to injured sightseers, look out for forest fires, redirect hikers around potentially dangerous areas, and protect an area's natural resources.

17 NATIONAL PARK SERVICE EMPLOYEE

WANT TO BE A PARK SERVICE RANGER? CHECK OUT FIVE OF THE MANY COOL PARKS IN THE U.S. YOU COULD CALL YOUR "OFFICE."

1 YELLOWSTONE NATIONAL PARK

Established in 1872, this was **AMERICA'S FIRST NATIONAL PARK.** It's home to grizzly bears, wolves, bison, elk, and the world's greatest concentration of geysers, including the famous Old Faithful, which erupts every hour or two and shoots water about 140 feet (43 m) into the air.

2 EVERGLADES NATIONAL PARK

The American Everglades in **SOUTH FLORIDA** are the largest subtropical wilderness in the United States and are chock-full of amazing wildlife, including manatees, bobcats, Florida panthers, crocodiles, alligators, wild pigs, and Burmese pythons.

3 MOUNT RUSHMORE

From 1927 until 1941, more than 400 workers sculpted the 60-foot (18-m)-high replicas of four U.S. presidents—George Washington, Thomas Jefferson, Theodore Roosevelt, and Abraham Lincoln—into the granite of the Black Hills near Keystone, **NORTH DAKOTA.**

4 GRAND CANYON

Located in **ARIZONA** and carved by the Colorado River, the Grand Canyon is more than 6,000 feet (1,829 m) deep at its deepest point and 18 miles (29 km) wide at its widest.

5 MAMMOTH CAVE

In **KENTUCKY**, you can take underground tours—complete with lots of bats!—in the world's longest cave system. More than 400 miles (644 km) have been explored.

FUN FACT!

The **LARGEST** national park in the United States is **WRANGELL-ST. ELIAS** National Park and Preserve in Alaska. It is bigger than the country Switzerland and equal in size to **SIX YELLOWSTONE NATIONAL PARKS!**

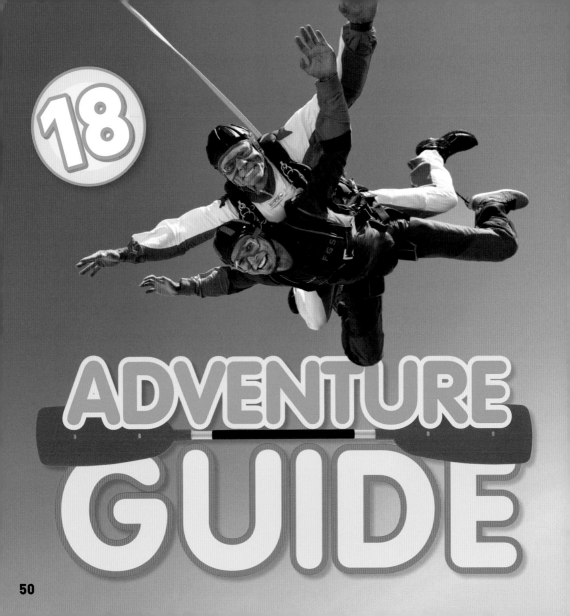

18

ADVENTURE
GUIDE

They **JUMP OUT OF PLANES** with a **PARACHUTE** strapped to their back, **CHARGE DOWN RUSHING RAPIDS** in rafts, zoom through **TREETOPS** on **ZIP LINES,** and lead groups on **INCREDIBLE EXPEDITIONS** in **BREATHTAKING WILDERNESS.** Adventure guides are **FUN-CHASING, THRILL-SEEKING NATURE LOVERS** who want to share their **PASSION** with other people.

51

19

PARTY Planner

From the THEME to the MUSIC to the FLOWERS to the CAKE, a party planner organizes every detail of a fun fiesta.

PROFESSIONAL
Bridesmaid

Though people have all sorts of weddings, one tradition is for the two people getting married to have a **WEDDING "PARTY."** These are the people who stand beside them as they recite their vows and **SUPPORT THEM** through the wedding process.

> A groom's attendants are often called *GROOMSMEN*, and a bride's are often called *BRIDESMAIDS.*

These days, there are companies that provide professional bridesmaids. **FOR THE RIGHT PRICE,** these individuals will **STAND BESIDE THE BRIDE** on her big day and **TAKE CARE OF BEHIND-THE-SCENE DETAILS** like party planning, dress fittings, and even peacekeeping between family members.

FUN FACT!

It's believed that the tradition of bridesmaids **BEGAN IN ANCIENT ROME** as a sort of **DECOY FOR EVIL SPIRITS.** The bridesmaids would dress the same as the bride to **CONFUSE EVIL SPIRITS** that might be looking to ruin the bride's happiness.

21 ANIMAL GROOMER

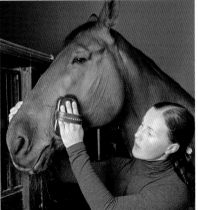

These are the **FOLKS** who help **FIDO** look **FANCY.**

They **trim** nails, **clean** ears and eyes, and sometimes even **add a bit of bling**, like a bow or a bandanna.

22

RECIPE TESTER

- You've seen the recipes on the back of cereal boxes or a bag of chocolate chips.
- How about the ones in magazines and cookbooks or on websites?

Each one of these recipes has to be tested to make sure the ingredients, measurements, and cook times are correct. The people who do this are recipe testers. Sometimes these individuals work in fancy, state-of-the-art kitchens; other times, they cook right out of their homes.

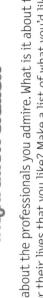

Inspiration station

Think about the professionals you admire. What is it about their jobs or their lives that you like? Make a list of what you'd like to have in your own life or job, as well as anything you wouldn't.

MOVIE TRAILER EDITOR

When the lights go down in a movie theater, everyone in the audience waits for the first trailer to fill the screen. Will there be ...

CAR CHASES?
EPIC BATTLES?
Silly slapstick?
Sweet romance?

Movie trailer editors are the people who create these trailers. When they receive a finished film, they pick out the very best bits and splice them together so that the audience understands what the movie's about. Then they add the perfect song or two. If the movie trailer editors have done a good job, no matter what genre of movie it is, you'll feel like it's a "must-see"!

23

PRIMATOLOGIST

24

There are MORE THAN 300 SPECIES of primates, including humans. The smallest species is the PYGMY MOUSE LEMUR, which can WEIGH AS LITTLE AS AN OUNCE (28 g). The largest species is the GORILLA, which can weigh MORE THAN 400 POUNDS (181 kg).

For some, primatology, or the **study of primates, is serious monkey business.**
(Get it? Monkey business? Because monkeys are primates ...)

ONE OF THE MOST FAMOUS PRIMATOLOGISTS IS JANE GOODALL (pictured here), WHO STUDIED CHIMPANZEES BY LIVING AMONG THEM IN THE FORESTS OF TANZANIA.

WiLd & wAcKy!

ICEBERG TRACKER

It's true: There's a **WHOLE DIVISION** of the U.S. **COAST GUARD** devoted to identifying, reporting, and **TRACKING ICEBERGS.** It's called the **INTERNATIONAL ICE PATROL.**

MEET DANIEL MORRISEY,
A MARINE SCIENCE TECHNICIAN IN THE U.S. COAST GUARD'S INTERNATIONAL ICE PATROL.

RECONNAISSANCE= MILITARY SURVEYING OF AN AREA FOR RESEARCH.

When was the International Ice Patrol formed?

The International Ice Patrol was formed as a response to the sinking of the RMS *Titanic* in 1912. After that tragedy, the international community came together to establish safety regulations preventing future maritime disasters. The United States was selected as the managing government of the Ice Patrol, and in the 100-plus years since, no vessel heeding the patrol's warnings has collided with an iceberg.

MARITIME = HAVING TO DO WITH THE SEA.

How has tracking icebergs changed over time?

In the beginning, we used Coast Guard cutters [a "cutter" is any Coast Guard vessel 65 feet (20 m) in length or greater], which would find the southeasternmost iceberg and then just drift with it. While on the scene with an iceberg, the cutter would make radio broadcasts to the vessels in the vicinity so they could avoid the iceberg. After World War II, we began using aircraft for visual reconnaissance. Then, in the 1980s, we expanded our use of aircraft by using airborne radar to search for icebergs. We are now in the process of testing and incorporating satellite reconnaissance.

What do you do once you spot an iceberg?

Whenever an iceberg is sighted, it is added to a database within our Iceberg Analysis and Prediction System. An iceberg drift and deterioration model is then run on the iceberg to predict how it'll melt and drift, to see where the iceberg will go. The results of this model are published daily on our iceberg warning products. The chart that we make is basically a map with a pink line on it. If vessels stay outside of that line, they won't come in contact with an iceberg.

Where do you monitor icebergs?

Generally, we monitor icebergs near the Grand Banks of Newfoundland, Canada. Everything below, or south of, the latitude line of 48 degrees north is considered the shipping lanes for vessels making trans-Atlantic voyages. Our primary concern is providing a warning to those vessels when there is a threat of icebergs.

Are you concerned about all icebergs or only ones of a certain size?

We monitor all icebergs of any size. Small

icebergs [of 49 to 197 feet (15 to 60 m)] and growlers [fewer than 49 feet (15 m)] tend to be the most dangerous to ships. Small icebergs are about the size of a moderate-size house, whereas growlers are closer to the size of a car or piano. The reason the smaller icebergs are more dangerous is because they tend to be more difficult to detect by ships both visually and with radar, and they will still do a lot of damage if struck by a vessel.

In the North Atlantic Ocean region, there tends to be a lot of poor weather. Whether there is fog, rain, snow, wind, or storms, when there are a lot of waves and white caps, it makes spotting the smaller icebergs difficult. Larger icebergs, while still a huge danger, are generally much easier to see visually and on radar.

What kinds of boats are usually traveling through these waters?

The vessels that frequent the areas that we monitor are trans-Atlantic cargo ships. Some of them carry hundreds of containers; others carry thousands of barrels of oil or dry goods. They're very large ships that weigh in at 300 tons (272 t) or more. At times, passenger ships will transit through the area. In fact, the *Queen Mary II*, a cruise ship capable of holding more than 2,600 passengers, regularly passes through the area, too.

How quickly do icebergs move?

Icebergs will move as fast as the wind and currents take them. If an iceberg is right in the core of the Labrador Current, it could drift as far as 25–30 nautical miles (46–56 km) a day! However, farther from this current, which brings icebergs south, the icebergs drift much more slowly.

What is your favorite part of your job?

I love going to Canada and flying around. Carrying out our mission while being deployed is a ton of fun. Also, we get to see the direct impact our work has when we create our iceberg warnings each day, documenting the icebergs we see or have reported to us. It's incredibly rewarding.

LABRADOR CURRENT = A COLD-WATER CURRENT IN THE NORTH ATLANTIC OCEAN THAT FLOWS SOUTH FROM THE ARCTIC OCEAN ALL THE WAY TO THE WARM GULF STREAM NEAR THE GRAND BANKS OF NEWFOUNDLAND.

26

ASTRO-
NOMER

SHOOTING STARS, BLACK HOLES, DWARF PLANETS, ORBITING ASTEROIDS, METEOR SHOWERS—

these are all in a day's (or night's) work for an astronomer. These scientists use math and physics to make discoveries, test theories, and conduct research about space and its celestial bodies.

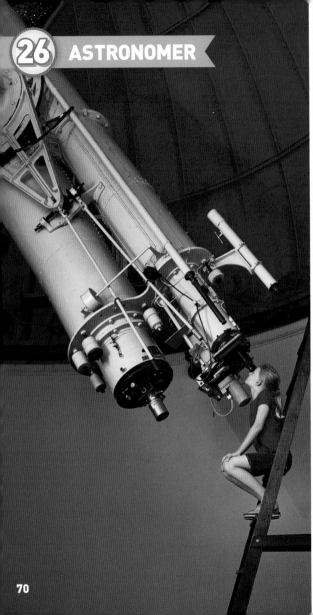

Many astronomers also get to use very cool, very high-powered telescopes. The biggest ones are housed in buildings all by themselves. To get the best visibility, they're placed on the top of high hills or mountains, in remote locations, far from the lights of cities or towns.

WANT TO SEE SOME **SERIOUS** STAR POWER? **CHECK OUT** THESE THREE **AWE-INSPIRING** TELESCOPES.

WHAT: The Keck Observatory
WHERE: Mauna Kea, Hawaii, U.S.A.
WOW: Built on the dormant Mauna Kea volcano, 17,796 feet (5,424 m) above sea level, are the twin Keck telescopes—the world's largest optical and infrared telescopes. Each telescope stands eight stories tall and weighs 300 tons (272 metric tons).

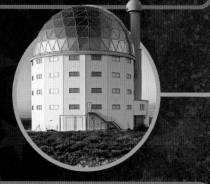

WHAT: The Southern African Large Telescope (SALT)
WHERE: The Northern Cape of South Africa
WOW: This is the largest single optical telescope in the Southern Hemisphere. Through it, scientists can view stars and galaxies that are a billion times too faint to be seen by the naked eye.

WHAT: The Hubble Telescope
WHERE: In space! This optical telescope was launched from Kennedy Space Center in 1990 to an altitude of about 340 miles (547 km) from Earth.
WOW: This telescope, which is roughly the length of a school bus and weighs about the same as two adult elephants, takes pictures of stars, planets, and galaxies as it orbits Earth at nearly 17,000 miles per hour (27,359 km/h).

PALEONTOLOGIST

Sort of like DIGGING DETECTIVES, paleontologists are looking for clues about PAST LIFE FORMS. They dig and chip and brush away layers of dirt, LOOKING FOR FOSSILS.

27

Paleontologists have FOUND FOSSILS that are BILLIONS OF YEARS OLD. And from these fossils, they're able to start piecing together an idea of what life was like back then—how those organisms lived, what they ate, what ate them— and HOW LIFE HAS CHANGED OVER TIME.

A FOSSIL IS ANY EVIDENCE OF PAST PLANT OR ANIMAL LIFE THAT HAS BEEN PRESERVED IN EARTH'S CRUST. Some examples are prehistoric insects that have been preserved in sap, fish skeletons, and the bones of dinosaurs.

However, even if the organic matter from the once-living thing no longer remains, sometimes there is still evidence to be found. One way this can happen is if a plant or animal is COVERED IN SEDIMENT AFTER IT DIES. The plant or animal may decay, but the IMPRESSION IT MADE IN THE DIRT MAY REMAIN.

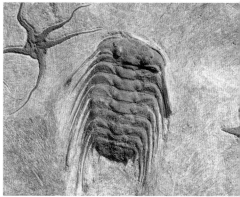

FUN FACT!

In 2002, scientists in England found the world's oldest **FOSSILIZED VOMIT!** It's believed to be from an **ICHTHYOSAUR,** a large marine mammal that lived more than **160 MILLION YEARS AGO.** Ichthyosaurs were related to land-dwelling dinosaurs and are believed to have looked **KIND OF LIKE A DOLPHIN,** but with a pointed snout full of sharp teeth.

28

ART
Conservationist

IN MANY ART MUSEUMS, THERE ARE WORKS THAT ARE HUNDREDS OF YEARS OLD. For example, Leonardo da Vinci began painting the *Mona Lisa* about 513 years ago. An art conservator's job is to keep the artwork in good condition and prevent it from fading, peeling, or cracking.

CONSERVATORS USE DIFFERENT PRESERVATION METHODS DEPENDING ON THE TYPE OF ART. One way artwork is protected is by keeping it in rooms where the humidity and temperature are carefully regulated. To restore an old painting, a conservator might repair a tear in the canvas, remove discolored varnish, or even retouch faded portions of the painting with new paint.

TO RESTORE AN OLD PIECE OF POTTERY, A CONSERVATOR MIGHT USE A VACUUM, SCALPEL, OR BRUSHES TO CLEAN THE CRACKS AND CREVICES. In some cases, an art piece might even need to be fumigated to get rid of any bugs or other critters that have taken up residence.

FUN FACT!

Using specialized scanners, **X-RAYS**, lasers, and microscopes, art professionals are able to **SEE WHAT'S BENEATH** the paintings we see. Sometimes there are **FIRST DRAFTS**, sketches, or even **ENTIRELY DIFFERENT PAINTINGS.**

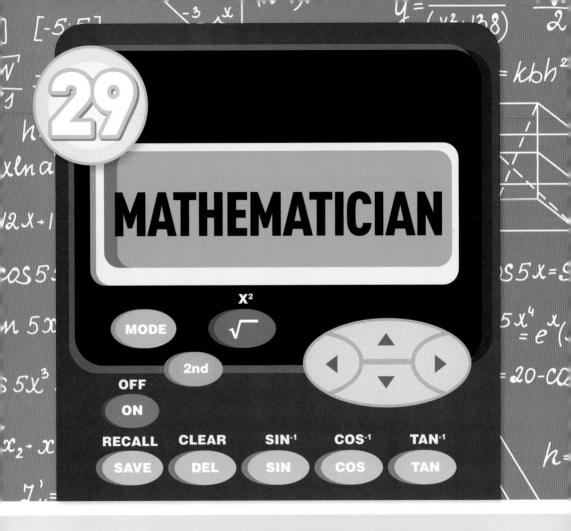

29

MATHEMATICIAN

Mathematicians use math and all of its theorems, formulas, and models to solve real-world problems.

MATH WHIZZES WANTED!

Here are five cool careers a mathematician might have.

① **METEOROLOGIST**

② **ECONOMIST**

③ **ARCHITECT**

④ **COMPUTER PROGRAMMER**

⑤ **TEACHER**

If you think you were born bad at math, THINK AGAIN!

Sure, some people are math geniuses, but most of us just have to work hard to figure it out. See, math isn't something you're born knowing, and it can definitely be a brain-tickling challenge. But, it is within your ability. If you think that you're "bad at math," make sure you didn't just give up trying before you understood it. With some hard work, patience, and dedication, you—yes, YOU!—can be good at math. Really.

MAKE-UP
Artist

30

There are the make-up artists who **accentuate people's beauty** with a bit of blush or a little lipstick.

There are others who **transform faces** by making people look like someone or something completely different. Special effects make-up artists might be tasked with making an actor look 100 years old, covered in tattoos, or suffering some gruesome injury. Through the magic of make-up, they can also turn humans into aliens, hobbits, or werewolves.

FUN FACT!

It took **SIX MAKE-UP ARTISTS** working together for **SEVEN HOURS** to transform Jennifer Lawrence into **MYSTIQUE** for the movie *X-MEN: FIRST CLASS*.

31

POLITICAL
Speechwriter

AN AMAZING SPEECH CAPTIVATES AN AUDIENCE. IT CAN INSPIRE, COMFORT, ENGAGE, AND MOTIVATE.

The right words can bring a crowd to its feet, get people cheering and applauding, and may even take their breath away. There is tremendous power in being able to communicate clearly what's important to you—your thoughts, your fears, your dreams, and your plans—with an audience.

Many politicians are gifted speakers, but even the best and the brightest work with professional speechwriters.

Speechwriters know a lot about politics, work well with people, and have an amazing way with words.

Together with the politician, a speechwriter helps figure out exactly what the message of a speech should be, who the audience will be, and the most moving, most effective way to communicate the desired ideas to that audience.

MEET *SHANNON WALKER.*

SHE'S AN ASTRONAUT. SHE TRAVELS TO OUTER SPACE FOR A LIVING.
I KNOW, RIGHT? THE COOLEST!

When Shannon Walker was four years old, she watched as two U.S. astronauts took the first steps ever to be taken on the moon. She knew then that she wanted to know more. It helped that she grew up in Houston, Texas, near the Johnson Space Center (NASA's center for human spaceflight), so she was always up on the latest happenings at NASA.

RENDEZVOUS = WHEN A SPACECRAFT APPROACHES ANOTHER SPACECRAFT OR A SPACE STATION AND GETS CLOSE ENOUGH TO SEE THEM OR EVEN ATTACH TO THEM (WHICH IS CALLED "DOCKING").

As a kid, what was it about becoming an astronaut that you thought was so cool?

It was the idea of going to other places, and that we were *here* and they were *there*. I loved that we had people in space and astronauts walking on the moon. Also, I wanted to be an explorer!

Knowing you wanted to be an astronaut, did you make a plan to reach your goal?

Even though I knew that I wanted to be an astronaut, I had no idea what that would take. When I was growing up, all of the astronauts began as military fighter pilots. And, since I was a little girl, and I didn't see any girls in the NASA Astronaut Corps, I thought maybe being an astronaut wasn't an option for me. Then, as I got older, women began being selected for NASA's Space Shuttle program, so I began to think it was more of a possibility. Also, I was always interested in math and science, which was good, because that's exactly what you need to study in school to be an astronaut.

So, what exactly does an astronaut do?

When we're in space, we conduct scientific experiments and collect data for the scientists on the ground. Or we work on maintaining or repairing our space station.

You spent six months on the International Space Station; what was that like?

Oh man, it was just so much fun! It really was. To get to the space station, I flew on the Russian Soyuz rocket from Kazakhstan, Russia. I was really fortunate because I was selected to fly as the copilot and was trained to do everything from launch, rendezvous, dock, undock, and fly back to Earth. It was really neat.

SPACEWALK = WHEN AN ASTRONAUT DOES AN ACTIVITY OUTSIDE THE SPACECRAFT WHILE IN SPACE.

Wow!

Also, while we were there, we did three spacewalks. I wasn't selected to do any of them personally, but I supported the spacewalks by operating the robotic arm. In addition to moving around hardware with the robotic arm, I also moved around my fellow crewmates with it while they were on their spacewalks.

What's the purpose of a spacewalk?

In the early days, we did a lot of spacewalks to actually build the space station. We would take parts up on the shuttle and then use the arm of the shuttle or the arm of the space station to connect the big pieces together. But it was still necessary to go outside and do a spacewalk to make all of the connections the robotic arm couldn't, like the electrical connections or fluid connections. During a spacewalk, the astronaut also makes sure that everything is put together properly. The space station has been operating for 15 years and parts eventually wear out and break, so these days, a lot of our spacewalks are done to repair equipment on the outside.

What part of going to space excited you or surprised you the most?

Well, launching on a rocket is extremely exciting. There's lots of noise and lots of vibrations—you really know you're going someplace and you're going someplace fast. But I think some of the interesting things are some of the more subtle ones, like how easy and quickly you adapt to living in space and how normal it feels to float out of your sleeping bag in the morning and float over to breakfast and then float on to start your day. You just get to float all day! It's a lot of fun and it feels quite normal after a while.

Is there anything you've done in space that you're most proud of?

All of it, really. But, some of the most interesting scientific studies, to me, are the ones we do to study the human body where we, the astronauts, become the test subjects. We provide samples or do certain activities for the experimenters on the ground so that they can see how the human body reacts in space.

What are some of the necessary skills or traits that someone needs to be an astronaut?

Well, you definitely need to be an explorer. You need to be curious about the world and the universe, you need to always be willing to learn more, and you should be excited to go to new places.

FUN FACT!

U.S. astronaut Scott Kelly spent **340 CONSECUTIVE DAYS** living in the International Space Station (from March 27, 2015 to March 1, 2016). During the flight, he made 5,000 trips around the Earth and **DRANK NEARLY 200 GALLONS** of drinking water made from **RECYCLED SWEAT AND URINE.**

❶ WHAT MIGHT SURPRISE PEOPLE ABOUT LIFE IN SPACE?

I get asked a lot of if we have cell phones in space. The answer is "No." But we do have email and phone communication, so we're able to stay connected with family and friends.

❷ WHAT'S SOMETHING THAT TOOK SOME GETTING USED TO?

In space, you're floating all the time, so to get to where you need to go, you have to push off the walls or the ceilings or the floor. An important lesson is figuring out how hard you need to push so you don't get hurt.

Because however hard you push off, when you get to where you need to go, you're going to have to stop yourself.

❸ WHAT DO YOU DO DURING YOUR DOWNTIME IN SPACE?

We're actually really busy, so we don't have a lot of free time. But, because we usually all have different assignments during the day, we typically have meals or watch movies together. And, there are some games you can play in space. We used to start at one end of the space station and push off and see how far we can get through the space station, without touching anything. We'd fly like Superman, avoiding all the obstacles along the way. That was always fun.

❹ WHAT'S YOUR FAVORITE PART OF BEING AN ASTRONAUT?

Being in space. That's my favorite part.

❺ ANY WORDS OF ADVICE FOR ASPIRING ASTRONAUTS?

Do well in school. Enjoy what you do. And, don't be afraid to try new things. You never know where life is going to take you. New experiences add to who you are as a person and they can open new doors for you.

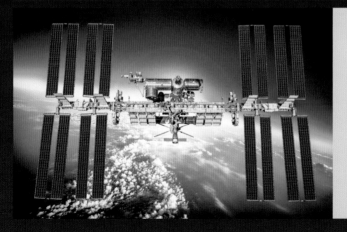

« What is the INTERNATIONAL SPACE STATION (ISS)?

It's a laboratory in space that orbits the Earth every 90 minutes. The ISS is about the width of a football field and has about as much space inside as a six-bedroom house. More than 222 crew members, from 18 countries, have visited the ISS to conduct research to learn more about science, Earth, space, and the universe. Want to see the ISS go past your house? You can grab a parent and check out NASA.gov for times when it will be visible where you live. The ISS is the second-brightest object in the night sky after the moon—you won't even need a telescope to spot it!

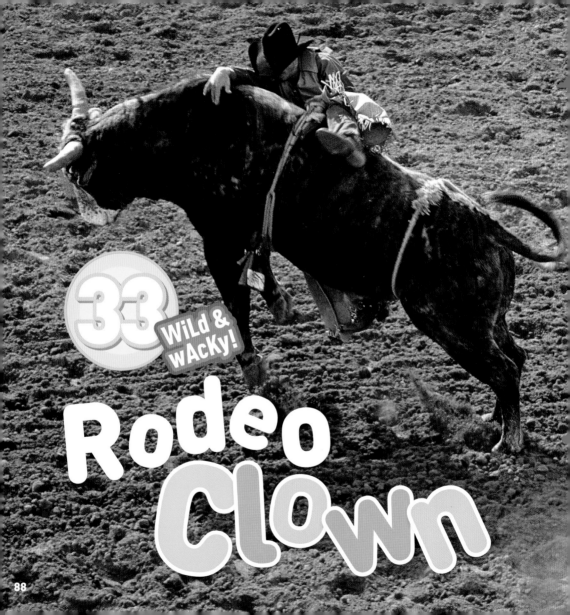

33

WiLd & wAcKy!

Rodeo
Clown

While part of their job is to entertain the crowd between events with skits, jokes, and tricks, the other part of their job is no laughing matter. Rodeo clowns, also known as bullfighters, are in the ring during bull-riding competitions to protect bull riders once they jump or are thrown from the bull. This often means that the rodeo clowns will **TRY TO DISTRACT THE BULL FROM CHARGING AND GOUGING A RIDER BY GETTING IT TO CHASE THEM INSTEAD.**

Oh, and one more thing—bulls can weigh a ton. That's 2,000 pounds (907 kg). That's as heavy as eight refrigerators! It's a **VERY DANGEROUS JOB, AND IT REQUIRES SERIOUS BRAVERY.**

THE GOAL FOR A BULL RIDER IS TO STAY ON A BUCKING BULL FOR EIGHT SECONDS BEFORE JUMPING OFF OR BEING THROWN.

FUN FACT!

A rodeo clown who uses a BARREL FOR PROTECTION from a charging bull is known as the "BARREL MAN." The barrels, which are big enough for the clowns to jump in and out of easily, are MADE OF ALUMINUM OR STEEL and are heavily padded for the clowns' safety.

Perfumer

To create scents for perfumes, candles, toiletries, and household products, perfumers must have more than a **GREAT SENSE OF SMELL.** They need to be innovative and creative so that they can dream up new fragrance combinations. And they must be **WELL VERSED IN CHEMISTRY** to be able to create the desired scent using just the right combination of chemical compounds. In fact, when a perfumer, also known as a "nose," has an idea for a fragrance, it will often first be written as a chemical equation before it's mixed up in a lab.

A PERFECT PERFUMER = 1 PART SENSITIVE SNIFFER + 1 PART DREAMER + 1 PART ARTIST + 1 PART CLEVER CHEMIST!

Pet Food TASTER

35

WiLd & wAcKy!

DOGS ARE GREAT AT LOTS OF THINGS— going for walks; rolling in strange, smelly things they find in the yard; and snuggling, though, hopefully, not in that order! But there's one thing at which dogs aren't so great, and that's being able to tell you, "I think this kibble needs a little more fish and a bit less carrot." Because, you see, dogs (and really all pets, for that matter) can't talk. So, to make sure they're giving your beloved Bowzer the healthiest, best-tasting food, **PET FOOD COMPANIES EMPLOY HUMANS TO TASTE THEIR PRODUCTS.** Um, no seconds for me, thanks!

93

36
FARRIER

Unlike humans, when horses need new shoes, they can't just hop in the car and head to the mall. Instead, they get a visit from a farrier. A farrier is a **PROFESSIONAL WHO PUTS SHOES ON HORSES.**

Many domesticated, or trained, horses walk, run, and work much more than wild horses. Some carry tourists for scenic trail rides or race at high speeds around tracks. Others carry law enforcement officers during long shifts on city streets or ranchers herding cattle from one pasture to another. All of this **ACTIVITY CAN BE TOUGH ON THEIR HOOVES,** which are made of keratin, just like human fingernails. Horses' **HOOVES CAN SPLIT OR BECOME TOO WORN DOWN** and, just like when you cut your fingernails too short, that hurts!

To protect horses' hooves from cracking or wear, humans started attaching curved metal shoes to their feet. Today, horseshoes are often **MADE OF STEEL** and can be applied with nails, which don't hurt the horses, or in some cases, adhesive.

FUN FACT!

Before a farrier puts new shoes on a horse, the professional shoer examines the horse's feet and legs to make sure they're healthy. Then the farrier uses special tools, including nippers and a hoof knife, to cut the hoof down to a healthy length. Next, a rasp, or large file, is used to smooth the bottom of the horse's hoof. Finally, the horseshoe is bent to fit the hoof before it's attached.

37 WOOD-WORKER

MEET ALEKSANDRA ZEE.

She creates geometric patterns out of wood that fit together to form funky wall hangings and tabletops.

"I have always been interested in **working with my hands,**" says Zee, who studied studio art in college. "But it wasn't until I got a job **building displays for a retail store** that I realized **I loved working with wood.**"

37

TODAY,

she works out of her studio in Oakland, California, U.S.A., and has turned her passion for woodworking into her full-time job.

What's your favorite tool?

My nail gun!

What's your favorite part of the woodworking process?

After I put the last nail in the frame, I set the piece against the brick wall in my studio and look at it. Each piece of artwork feels like a journey, and looking at the finished product is always so rewarding.

How do you come up with new ideas?

I get new ideas every day—from conversations, the clouds, or just walking down the street. I'm most inspired outside. Feeling the power of Mother Nature always awakens my creativity.

What traits does a woodworker need?

There's a saying, "Measure twice, cut once." A woodworker must be patient with themselves and their material. Also, you need tough skin, literally and figuratively. And, to create original artwork, you have to be authentic to yourself.

What do you love most about being a woodworker?

Wood is a raw and natural material, and I feel deeply connected to working with it. I feel one with myself and with the world around me when I am creating and making art with my hands. I wouldn't have it any other way.

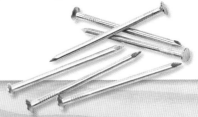

"A lot of what I do now is **self-taught,**" says Zee. **"Practice really does make perfect,** and the more I make, the better my work becomes."

38

FASHION
Designer

It all **STARTS WITH AN IDEA,** a dream of how a piece of clothing might look or feel or fit or flutter. The next step is to be able to **COMMUNICATE YOUR VISION.** You might describe it in words, sketch it, or find pictures that express your inspiration. In her early days, designer Vera Wang would even sketch her ideas on napkins.

Then, you turn your **THOUGHTS INTO THREADS** by either sewing the garment yourself or working with someone who sews to get it made. Finally, you get to celebrate the moment when someone wears your work.

Voilà!

39 MARINE Biologist

MARIANA FUENTES.

FUENTES HAS HAD AN EXPERIENCE VERY FEW OTHERS HAVE—WHEN SHE WAS 17, SHE GOT A HICKEY FROM A MANTA RAY.

GROWING UP, SHE THOUGHT SHE WANTED TO BE A LARGE ANIMAL VETERINARIAN AND LIVE IN AFRICA. But that all changed when she was 16 and got chased by an elephant on safari. "I knew then and there that wasn't for me," she says.

The next year, on a trip to the Cayman Islands, she visited a manta ray feeding area. It's there that she got the hickey (a mark made by the suction from the ray trying to feed) and realized her true calling. "I was fascinated and wanted to know more about the ray's behavior," says Fuentes. "I asked the marine biologists on board several questions, and after that trip, I knew I was going to be a marine biologist."

TODAY, SHE FOCUSES HER RESEARCH AND CONSERVATION EFFORTS ON MARINE TURTLES, and she teaches students about them as a professor at a university.

HOW DID YOU CHOOSE TO FOCUS ON TURTLES?

During my first year as an undergraduate, I did an internship at Projeto Tamar, a sea turtle protection group in Brazil. That's where I became captivated by them. Sea turtles are warriors. When I learned the multiple threats and obstacles that sea turtles face at every life stage—out of thousands of hatchlings, usually only one lives to maturity—it made me appreciate every turtle that I encountered. Since then, I've wanted to work at places that seek to conserve and manage sea turtles through community involvement and education.

WHAT DID YOU STUDY TO BECOME A MARINE BIOLOGIST?

In high school, I took an introductory field course in marine biology. Then, in college, I majored in marine biology and environmental sciences. And because a lot of my work is done out in the field—which in this case is actually the ocean—I've also been certified in scuba diving, driving boats, and first aid.

WHAT KINDS OF FIELD-WORK DO YOU DO?

I have worked in several countries, including the United States, Brazil, Barbados, Vanuatu, Australia, Madagascar, and Kenya! My fieldwork varies depending on the particular project, but it can include anything from monitoring nesting turtles, deploying temperature data-loggers, and interviewing managers to scuba diving and conducting beach-elevation models. My days are very diverse, which is one of the things that I love about my job.

WHAT'S ONE OF YOUR FAVORITE PARTS OF BEING A MARINE BIOLOGIST?

I love working with and meeting people with diverse backgrounds from around the globe. I travel a lot for my work, attending conferences and conducting fieldwork, so I get to meet all sorts of people who inspire me, from curious kids on remote islands to devoted resource managers, dedicated volunteers, and smart academics.

WHAT'S **ONE THING YOU NEED** TO BE A **MARINE BIOLOGIST?**

It helps if you're **CURIOUS** and interested in why and **HOW THINGS WORK.**

HISTORICAL

Do you **LOVE HISTORY** and have a **FLARE FOR THE DRAMATIC?** You might enjoy being a historical reenactor. These dedicated historians perform for an audience by talking, dressing, eating, dancing, and fighting in a manner authentic to the time period they're reenacting. The goal is to teach people about history and give them a taste of what life was like at the time.

Historical reenactors act out famous events like the **SALEM WITCH TRIALS** and the **BATTLE OF GETTYSBURG**, as well as offer a glimpse into what everyday life was like in a certain place during a particular time, such as **COLONIAL WILLIAMSBURG** or Europe during the medieval period.

SO DUST OFF YOUR TRICORNERED HAT AND SAVE ROOM FOR SOME PORRIDGE AND TURKEY DRUMSTICKS!

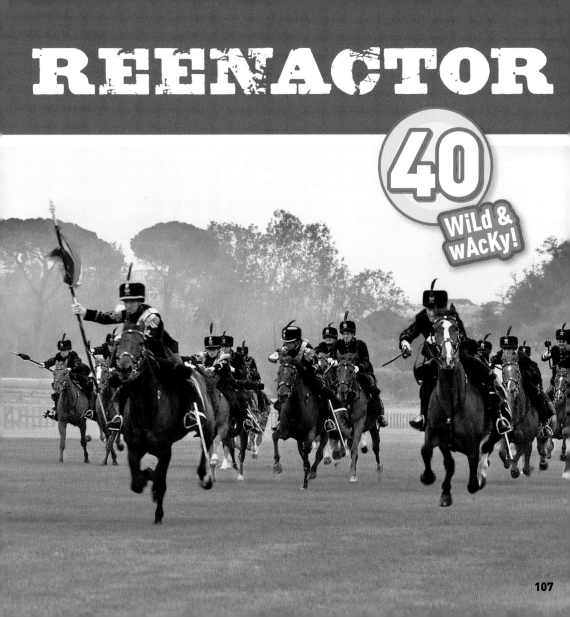

REENACTOR

40

WiLd & wAcKy!

41

PUBLICIST

When you love something, do you want to **shout about it from the ROOFTOPS?**

Do you want everyone to know **how AMAZING it is?**

PUBLICISTS make sure PEOPLE KNOW about their CLIENTS OR PRODUCTS. These could be a new restaurant, store, singer, or candy bar. Companies, as well as people, hire publicists to get them attention from the media (also known as publicity). Publicists work to get magazines and websites to write about a product, they try to get TV shows to cover it, and they aim to get people talking about it.

42 CIA ANALYST

The Central Intelligence Agency (CIA) protects the United States by **investigating security risks** and gathering information about potential threats. Sometimes, to do that, CIA analysts have to carry out **covert, or secret, operations.** Then they present their findings to government leaders, who create a plan to **keep Americans safe.**

inspiration station

Do you want to work in an office? In a laboratory? Outdoors? ... Do you like to work alone? Or on a team? ... Do you want to work in a city? Or somewhere rural?

Sometimes thinking about the day-to-day of how you want your life to feel can point you in exciting directions career-wise.

Oh! And don't worry if you don't have all the answers now. Trying stuff out to see what you like and what you don't like is a fun and important part of the journey.

Cranberry Farmer

43

There are all sorts of farms—Christmas trees, flowers, coffee beans, cattle, even pop-corn. One unique kind of farm is a cranberry farm. Like strawberries, cranberries grow on low-lying, trailing vines. Unlike strawberries, cranberry vines thrive in peat bogs.

PEAT BOG = A TYPE OF MARSHY, ACIDIC SOIL MADE OF DECOMPOSED PLANTS AND VEGETABLES.

1. When it's time to harvest the cranberries, the bog is flooded with about 18 inches (46 cm) of freshwater. Then the farmer uses a big piece of equipment called a water reel (nicknamed the eggbeater) to loosen the berries from their vines.

2. After the berries pop off the vines, they float to the surface of the bog, where the farmer gathers them together.

3. Next, the cranberries are loaded onto a truck and sent off to become juice or sauce or any other of the many cranberry products.

SOCIAL

WORKER

Social workers help people when they need it most.

They help families who may have lost their home, adults who have lost their jobs, people suffering from physical or mental illness, and so much more. Their aim is to equip people with the tools and services they need to live happy, healthy, productive lives.

44

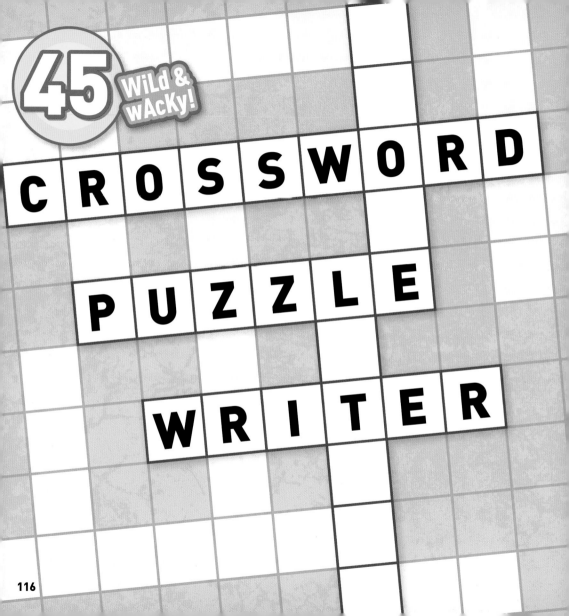

You may never have thought about it before, but someone actually creates the crossword puzzles you see in newspapers and magazines. In fact, there's quite an art to it. The people who do it enjoy thinking about words and coming up with clever clues—and getting all of that to fit together just so is like mental acrobatics. It takes an incredibly smart and patient person to write crossword puzzles. But the feeling you get when you see someone poring over a puzzle you created? One word, seven letters. A-W-E-S-O-M-E.

USE THE CLUES TO FIGURE OUT THE RIGHT WORD, THEN FILL IN THE BOXES.

Across

2. Another name for a crossword puzzle writer.

4. Unless you're an expert puzzler, it's best to use one of these when filling one out.

5. A crossword puzzle writer must be passionate about these.

Down

1. A crossword puzzle writer must have an extensive _____.

3. Not only must crossword puzzle writers think of cool words to fill their puzzles, they must also think of creative _____.

A PUZZLER'S PUZZLE

FUN FACT!

The crossword puzzle editor for the *New York Times*, **WILL SHORTZ**, is the **ONLY PERSON IN THE WORLD** to hold a college degree in **ENIGMATOLOGY**, the study of puzzles.

ANSWERS: 1. vocabulary; 2. constructor; 3. clues; 4. pencil; 5. words

TREE HOUSE BUILDER

IF YOU'VE EVER BEEN IN A TREE HOUSE—

A FORT, SOMETIMES 50 FEET (15 M) OFF THE GROUND, IN A TREE—YOU KNOW HOW COOL ONE CAN BE. BUT YOU KNOW SOMETHING EVEN COOLER THAN GETTING TO PLAY IN A TREE HOUSE? BEING THE PERSON WHOSE FULL-TIME JOB IT IS TO DESIGN AND BUILD THEM.

Tree houses can range from pretty basic to super swanky. The more elaborate structures can have multiple floors, spiral staircases, rope bridges, heat and electricity, wraparound porches, hot tubs, and pretty much anything else you could imagine. Of course, luxury comes at a price. These tricked-out tree houses can cost anywhere from $9,000 to hundreds of thousands of dollars.

47

GRAPHIC DESIGNER

If you've ever looked at a logo or a movie poster and thought, **Wow, *that's cool!*,** you were admiring the work of a graphic designer. A graphic designer is an artist who plans and designs the layout of words and images to communicate an idea or message visually— either on a computer or by hand.

CHECK OUT THESE FIVE EXAMPLES OF
EYE-CATCHING GRAPHIC DESIGN.

1. Book Covers

2. Cereal Boxes, Candy Wrappers and Soda Bottles

3. T-shirt Designs

4. Web Design

VOLCANOLOGIST

A **geologist** is a scientist who studies Earth and the materials it's made of, such as rocks and soil. **VOLCANOLOGISTS** are geologists who specialize in the **study of volcanoes.** They travel to dormant and active volcanoes to **conduct research** and **take samples and measurements.** Not only do they want to understand how and **why volcanoes erupt,** they also try to **predict** when a volcano **might erupt next,** in order to **protect the people who live nearby.**

DOCUMENTARY

A documentary is a **NONFICTION MOVIE**, which means it's based on **REAL FACTS**, **REAL LIFE**, and **REAL PEOPLE**. The purpose of a documentary is to give audiences an **IN-DEPTH LOOK** at a subject to teach them about it. So what sorts of subjects do documentaries cover? Anything and everything. Really. From **DOG SHOWS** and **DANCE CONTESTS** to **SPELLING BEES** and **BOY BANDS**.

FILMMAKER

◀ Legendary filmmakers, conservationists, and National Geographic Explorers-in-Residence Beverly and Dereck Joubert film elephants in the field.

FUN FACT!

The filmmakers who made the Academy Award-winning documentary *The March of the Penguins* spent **13 MONTHS IN ANTARCTICA** filming emperor penguins. They used **SLEDS** to carry their heavy equipment across the snow, and, because it was so cold—it got down to **-104°FAHRENHEIT** (-76°C)!— and the wind was so strong— up to 200 mph (322 km/h)!—the film crew would wear **SIX LAYERS OF CLOTHING** and sometimes could only stay outside for a few hours at a time.

HURRICANE HUNTER

50 WiLd & wAcKy!

When most people hear that a hurricane is headed their way, they get as far away as possible. The hurricane hunters of the U.S. Air Force Reserve, officially known as the 53rd Weather Reconnaissance Squadron, not only fly toward hurricanes, however, they fly *into* them!

These brave and highly trained pilots fly into tropical storms and hurricanes to get information about a storm that will help meteorologists make more accurate forecasts. They measure air temperature within the storm, wind speed, and the barometric pressure at the eye of the storm. They also observe the wind's direction and determine the exact latitude and longitude of the eye. These measurements help meteorologists determine where exactly the storm is, when it might make landfall, its strength, and whether it's getting weaker or stronger.

One must-have for a hurricane hunter? A high turbulence threshold.

A HURRICANE HUNTER'S HELPER

One instrument hurricane hunters use to collect data during a storm is called a **dropsonde.** This is a little tube attached to a square-cone parachute that is dropped from the plane to gather data as it falls to the ocean. The tube is filled with sensors that measure air pressure, temperature, humidity, wind speed, and wind direction, as well as a radio transmitter that sends that information back to the airplane.

FLORAL
designer

51

Sure, you need to know your chrysanthemums from your ranunculus and your peonies from your snapdragons, but if you love flowers, being surrounded by **beautiful, fragrant blooms** is pretty **scent-sational!** Floral designers are **artists** who create arrangements to **express all sorts of emotions**—sympathy, remorse, friendship, love, and celebration.

That's some serious flower power.

There are so many amazing possibilities for your life. You just have to dare to dream them first.

. . . .

"Every great dream begins with a dreamer. Always remember, you have within you the strength, the patience, and the passion to reach for the stars and change the world."

—— Harriet Tubman

ROBOTICS ENGINEER

Robots are machines that help humans do their jobs. Robotic engineers are the people who use their expertise in math, science, and technology to make robots. Some robots need a human to tell them what to do; others are programmed to act and respond on their own.

Robots are used in many different ways, in many different fields. NASA uses robots to explore outer space by going places and doing things that humans can't. Robots can stock shelves in warehouses, install car parts on assembly lines, vacuum floors, assist doctors during surgery, and even help to safely detonate bombs.

FRIENDS, ROMANS, COUNTRYMEN, LEND ME YOUR GEARS!

52

ICE
SCULPTOR

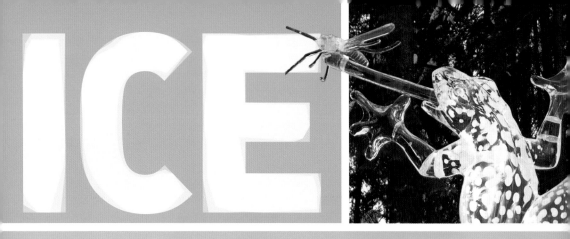

WHEN MOST ARTISTS CREATE A MASTERPIECE, they don't have to worry about it disappearing a few hours later. But when your art is made of ice, melting is an occupational hazard.

Meet Heather Brice. She and her husband, Steve, are **world-champion ice sculptors.** Though Brice studied bronze and wood sculpture in art school, it wasn't until she gave ice sculpting a go that she discovered her true **passion.** Once she began slicing that ice, she was hooked.

WHAT DO YOU DO TO IMPROVE YOUR SKILLS? I never stop practicing. I'm fortunate that from the beginning, I've been learning from the best—my husband, Steve. Also, the competitions have really helped me. Teams are given a time limit and a specific quantity of ice—so you can't just keep starting over if you mess up.

53

WHAT'S YOUR FAVORITE THING ABOUT BEING AN ICE SCULPTOR?
The competitions! They're a mix of sculpting, physical endurance, collaborating, and sharing my passion for ice sculpting.

DO YOU HAVE A FAVORITE SCULPTURE THAT YOU'VE WORKED ON?
One of my favorites was one that Steve and I created for the World Championships in Fairbanks, Alaska, U.S.A. It was based on the Grimm fairy tale "The Lion and the Mouse." Our sculpture was called "A Little Help" and had two mice on a broken branch pulling a thorn out of the lion's paw.

WHAT'S SOMETHING PEOPLE MIGHT NOT KNOW ABOUT ICE SCULPTING?
Because ice is translucent, it's difficult to photograph. Having different, distinctive textures can help the details to show up better in photos. And, since ice sculptures are temporary, it's very important to get a good photo of the finished piece.

WHAT SKILLS DOES AN ICE SCULPTOR NEED?
It's definitely an advantage to be skilled at drawing, and it's important to love art and be focused, determined, organized, and strong. Oh, and good tools!

DETECTIVE

As a solver of mysteries, a detective looks for clues and collects evidence to find out what exactly happened and who or what was involved.

mermaid

FUN FACT!

CHRISTOPHER COLUMBUS was one of many sailors who **CLAIMED TO HAVE SEEN MERMAIDS** during an ocean voyage. But, in reality, historians think what he and the other sailors thought were mermaids were actually **MANATEES.**

SINCE 1947, in Weeki Wachee Springs, FLORIDA, U.S.A., underwater performers dressed as mermaids have glided through crystal-clear spring water for audiences in the "MERMAID THEATER." The mermaids breathe through UNDERWATER AIR TUBES and then hold their breath for long stretches of time as they perform SYNCHRONIZED SWIMMING routines, EAT AND DRINK UNDERWATER, and put on shows like *The Little Mermaid* and *Fish Tails*.

VETERINARY ACUPUNCTURIST

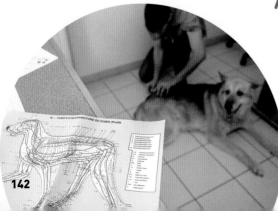

Acupuncture is a traditional form of Chinese medicine in which tiny needles are placed in the skin tissue to stimulate nerves, increase blood flow, and promote pain relief and healing in the body.

I HOPE THEY'RE NOT TURNING ME INTO A COW KABOB!

When your patient's a cow, you may not be able to get it to hop up on the exam table, but other than that, the treatment a veterinary acupuncturist gives to an animal is very similar to the treatment given to humans.

FORENSIC

57

THIS **SUPER-INTERESTING JOB** IS A **BLEND** OF **PSYCHOLOGY** AND **THE LAW.** A FORENSIC PSYCHOLOGIST IS A **LICENSED PSYCHOLOGIST** WHO APPLIES THE **STUDY** OF **PSYCHOLOGY** TO **LEGAL MATTERS.**

PSYCHOLOGIST

So, for example, a forensic psychologist might interview someone who's been **convicted of a crime** to determine whether the individual suffers from a **mental illness.** If the person or someone else involved in the trial is mentally ill, a forensic psychologist might **speak to the jury** about what that diagnosis means, how it might affect the person's life, whether it has an **effect on the accusations,** and whether it's a good idea for the person to speak on the witness stand.

If a psychological topic, like memory, becomes a **key part of the case,** forensic psychologists can also use their expertise to **explain the science** behind it to the jury and how it applies to the case.

58 Nutritionist

LIMAS AND TOMATOES AND BROCCOLI, OH MY!

Nutritionists are **experts** in **food** and **nutrition.** They help people find just the **right foods** to eat to feel their **healthiest, happiest,** most **energetic selves.**

JOURNALIST

A big part of being a journalist is being **curious,** asking good **questions,** and then having the **persistence** to find the answers to those questions. A journalist's job is to find information about issues that are **important or interesting** to readers and then **communicate** that information clearly, honestly, and **without** **bias.** There's **no topic off-limits** for journalists. They write about everything from people, places, and politics to Hollywood, homes, and health.

59

WHERE DO JOURNALISTS WORK?

Magazines
Websites
Newspapers
TV News
Radio Stations

BIAS = YOUR PERSONAL OPINIONS OR PREJUDICES.

COMPETITIVE EATER

60

WiLd & wAcKy!

It might not be the healthiest job, but professional eaters can make big bucks by winning competitions. From hot dogs and chicken wings to hamburgers and apple pies, competitive eaters stuff themselves with as much as they can in the allotted time, without "reversal" (also known as vomiting). Ugh! And you thought you felt full after Thanksgiving dinner!

FUN FACT!

Competitive eating superstar **JOEY CHESTNUT** holds the record for **MOST TWINKIES EATEN** in six minutes. So how many did he scarf down? **121!**

HERE, NATIONAL GEOGRAPHIC KIDS STAFF MEMBER HILARY ANDREWS COMPETES IN THE WORLD-FAMOUS NATHAN'S HOT DOG EATING CONTEST IN CONEY ISLAND, ON JULY 4, 2016.

JOEY CHESTNUT (PICTURED HERE, CENTER) WON THE 2016 NATHAN'S HOT DOG EATING CONTEST (SEEN ABOVE) BY EATING 70 HOT DOGS AND BUNS IN 10 MINUTES—THE MOST EVER AT THE COMPETITION.

BRAIN
surgeon

A NEUROSURGEON is a doctor who specializes in surgery of the brain, spinal cord, and peripheral nervous system.

61

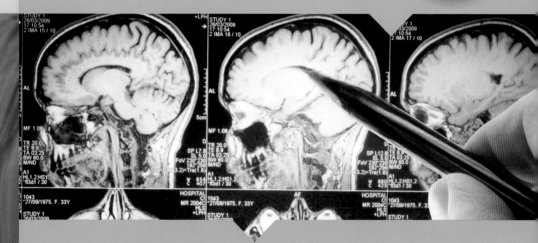

Neurosurgeons, at the very least, attend school for **14** years after high school *(and some for up to 20 years)* before they ever perform surgery. Not only do these **highly specialized** surgeons need to be incredibly smart, they also need to be able to expertly perform **incredibly detailed work** with their hands.

153

62 WiLd & wAcKy!

SIGN
SPINNER

FORGET BILLBOARDS

Sign spinners, also known as human directionals, stand on street corners and perform tricks with surfboard-size signs. They DANCE, TWIRL their signs, and even TOSS them into the air. To catch the eye of passersby, sign spinners have to be equally ATHLETIC and ENTHUSIASTIC. The best spinners receive training to improve their skills and have a personality for performing. Sign me up!

63 Landscape ARCHITECT

Lawn

From parks and playgrounds to rooftop gardens and golf courses, landscape architects design outdoor spaces by bringing together the natural environment, such as grass, plants, and trees, and manufactured elements, such as benches, gazebos, and greenhouses.

64

YOU MIGHT BE A **MOTIVATIONAL SPEAKER** in the making. Motivational speakers share stories about their personal history, or their particular INSIGHT, in an effort to INSPIRE others.

DO YOU HAVE A MESSAGE THAT THE WORLD WILL WANT TO HEAR? A thought or an idea that will motivate people to be stronger, braver, kinder, happier, and more authentic?

MOTIVATIONAL SPEAKER

inspiration station

Is there a career that you're interested in? To find out more about it, ask people in that field if you can interview them, or even shadow them for a day. What's a typical day like for them? What did they study in school to prepare for their career? How did they get to where they are? What do they love about their job? What don't they like?

Do you live to sketch?

Do you love to doodle?

illustrator

65

An ILLUSTRATOR is an artist who draws or paints pictures.

So what are some of the things an illustrator illustrates?
Wrapping Paper • CHILDREN'S BOOKS • Coffee Mugs • T-SHIRTS • Album Covers • DIAGRAMS IN SCIENCE TEXTBOOKS • Posters • COMIC BOOKS

A MINNIE MOUSE AT DISNEYLAND GETS INTO CHARACTER TO ADD MAGIC, WHIMSY, AND FUN TO PEOPLE'S DAY!

99 AMUSEMENT PARK ACTOR

WHEN YOU WORK AT AN AMUSEMENT PARK, YOU MIGHT SPEND YOUR DAYS AS MICKEY MOUSE OR MR. POTATO HEAD, SPONGEBOB OR SNOW WHITE. But getting to play one of these iconic characters doesn't come without rules. Once you put on the costume, there's no eating, sitting down, or chatting on your cell phone. You have to talk like your character, move like your character, and behave like your character. And, yes, it can get super steamy inside that heavy suit, but once you see the smiles your waves and hugs bring, it'll all be worth it!

163

67

Smoke-
JUMPER

A wildland fire, or wildfire, is one that happens in an area of combustible vegetation, such as a forest or dry grassland. Because there's a large area of highly flammable material, these fires tend to be very large and spread very quickly. Wildland firefighters are highly skilled firefighters who have been trained to fight this particular type of fire.

Smokejumpers are wildland firefighters who parachute out of small planes to fight fires, often in very remote locations.

Once smokejumpers jump from the plane and land near a fire, the supplies they need to fight the fire, as well as a 48-hour supply of food and water, are dropped from the plane to them by parachute.

Smokejumpers must be experienced at fighting wildfires, be in tip-top shape, and stay calm in stressful situations. They also receive lots of specialized training, including how to steer a parachute, how to use a chainsaw and compass, and how to climb trees in case they get stuck in one when parachuting into an area.

68 sign

LANGUAGE

INTERPRETER

To say "thank you" in sign language, bring the tips of your dominant hand toward your lips or chin and then, keeping your hand flat, bring your hand forward and downward toward the person you are thanking.

Sign language is used by **deaf and hard-of-hearing individuals** around the world. It is a language that uses signs made by **moving the hands** and using **facial expressions and body movements to communicate** as opposed to sound. In the United States, sign language interpreters must be fluent in American Sign Language (ASL).

Sign language interpreters help hearing and deaf or hard-of-hearing individuals communicate with each other. Interpreters might accompany deaf or hard-of-hearing students to school to facilitate communication between teachers and other students, or an interpreter might go with an adult to a doctor's appointment or the bank. A sign language interpreter might even interpret what a politician or official is saying to a crowd by standing beside the individual and signing.

CONSERVATION
Biologist

KRITHI KARANTH,

CONSERVATION BIOLOGIST AND NATIONAL GEOGRAPHIC EXPLORER.

"I HAD A PRETTY UNUSUAL CHILD-HOOD," SAYS KARANTH. "My dad's a tiger biologist, and he would take me with him to visit parks. I spent a lot of time watching animals and just hanging out with him."

As a conservation biologist, Karanth deals with how wild animals and humans interact in India. "So many of the challenges with animals are also about people," says Karanth. "If you're not able to solve people's problems, then you're not going to be able to help animals in the long run."

In India, 97 percent of the land is set aside for human use, so there is only about 3 percent left for nature. Because there isn't a lot of space left for wildlife, humans and animals often end up on each other's turf.

Karanth studies the conflicts between people and animals. For example, conflict can occur when an animal eats a farmer's crops or kills livestock. Sadly, sometimes people are injured, or even killed, trying to chase an animal away. When this happens, people may retaliate by poisoning or hurting the animals.

Through her work, Karanth is trying to build people's tolerance for wildlife so that they can coexist.

She took her first trip to the jungle when she was **1 YEAR OLD.**

She spotted her first leopard when she was **2 YEARS OLD.**

She tagged along on her first tiger-tracking expedition when she was **8 YEARS OLD.**

What did you study in school?

CONSERVATION = THE PRESERVATION, PROTECTION, OR RESTORATION OF THE NATURAL ENVIRONMENT, NATURAL ECOSYSTEMS, VEGETATION, AND WILDLIFE.

I grew up in India, so you kind of study everything. Then, as an undergraduate at the University of Florida, I started out in microbiology. But I quickly realized that I didn't like chemistry. That's when I switched into geography and environmental science. Eventually, I decided to pursue conservation during my master's degree at Yale University.

Has there been something that you've studied that's been most useful to you in your work?

What's interesting about being a conservation biologist is that you have to be interested in many different subjects. I love biology, I love geography, I love history, I love math, and I have a job that actually lets me dip into all four of those. Every project that I do, I'm constantly learning new things and collaborating with a wide range of people, like political scientists, economists, and technology experts. It's great fun.

What's your favorite part of what you do?

My absolute favorite part is spending time in any national park. Getting the opportunity to be out in the forest, when I see an animal or even when I don't see an animal, I'm happy.

Is there something you've done that you're most proud of?

Yes, it's a program we just recently launched. We did this big research project where we interviewed nearly 2,000 families from five tiger reserves in Karnataka, India, about their experiences of conflict with wildlife.

Some lost their sugarcane to a herd of elephants, while others' cows were killed by leopards or tigers. Occasionally, people were injured while they were chasing animals away, and very, very rarely, people were killed by tigers or elephants.

The hope is that by providing people with the help they need to get compensated for their losses, they'll be more tolerant to wildlife and won't retaliate against them. So, while this project started as a science project, it's now using technology to help conservation.

Of all the things I've done—and I've done a lot—I'm most proud of this project because I feel like it's actually making a difference in the world.

One of our big findings was that the people often don't file for compensation for their losses. They're entitled to it and the government has money to give them, but they're so frustrated with the process that few people are filing.

But, during our research, I noticed that regardless of how poor the people were, they all had mobile phones. So, I got the idea to use mobile technology to address this issue. Last year, we launched a 1-800 number. We advertised it by word of mouth and by sticking pamphlets around each of the villages.

Since we started the project, called WildSeve, we've helped roughly 3,700 families with filing for compensation. When someone calls, we have field staff who document what's happened and file the paperwork with the government.

70 WiLd & wAcKy!

EM♥JI ARTIST

While it may be hard to imagine a world without **emojis,** they're a relatively new phenomenon. And they didn't just appear out of thin air. They **were invented by a man in Japan, SHIGETAKA KURITA, in the late 1990s.** In fact, he sketched the very first emoji designs by hand using pencil and paper.

The simple little colorful drawings became a huge hit in Japan.

Then, in 2007, Apple and Google realized that if they were going to succeed at selling smartphones in Japan, they needed to create emojis for their devices. So, designers and programmers got to work creating the emojis we know and 🖤 today.

The word "emoji" is a Japanese word that loosely means **"small digital image or icon that expresses an idea or emotion."** The word, though, didn't become known outside of Japan until about 2011, when Apple made the emoji keyboard available on North American iPhones.

FUN FACT!

In 2015, this emoji (right), nicknamed face with tears of joy, was used the most around the world. That same year, the Oxford Dictionaries named it their "Word of the Year."

COMEDIAN

These funny folks don't mind being laughed at. In fact, they love it. They perform stand-up on stages, write silly scenes for TV shows and movies, act in online videos, host podcasts, and sometimes sing—all in the hope of making people happy and getting a laugh.

inspiration station

Be honest about who you are and what makes you happy.

"Your time is limited so don't waste it living someone else's life. Don't let the noise of others' opinions drown out your own inner voice. And most important, have the courage to follow your heart and intuition."

—Steve Jobs

Orchestra Musician

72

This job is the total pits—but in a good way! These talented musicians play their instruments during shows and performances from a lowered area in the front of the stage called an orchestra pit. The music accompanies a show, perhaps while a performer sings, during a big dance number or scene change, or sometimes to punctuate a dramatic moment (hello cymbals!). Broadway, here we come!

73

Callig

These artists specialize in decorative handwriting, which they create with a pen or brush. You might see their work on

rapher

book covers, coffee mugs, greeting cards, T-shirts, or even covering the wall of your favorite restaurant.

PEACE CORPS

The Peace Corps is a U.S. federal GOVERNMENT AGENCY, founded in 1961, that sends qualified Americans around the world to HELP PEOPLE IN NEED.

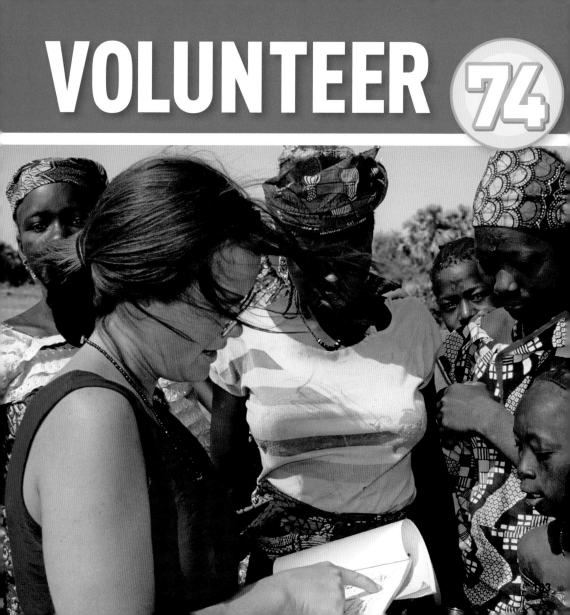

VOLUNTEER 74

MEET LESHIA HANSEN.

Hansen is a former Peace Corps volunteer. When she first heard about the Peace Corps in high school, she was determined to get involved. She loved learning about other cultures and traveling internationally, so to her, this job made perfect sense.

While an undergraduate, Hansen decided she wanted to become a nurse, so that she could help people. Once she earned her nursing degree, she studied public health before signing up to serve in the Peace Corps with her husband, Matthew Bruneel.

What was the project that you worked on like?

I served in Cambodia, in the northwest corner of the country, as a community health educator at a government-run health center. The center serves 24 different villages with about 2,500 residents total. I worked on a variety of projects. I helped educate pregnant mothers about how to have a healthy pregnancy and how to care for an infant. I also educated mothers with young children about good nutrition practices, and I'd monitor their children's weight to make sure they were growing up healthy.

I'd go with health center staff to vaccinate and address the health concerns of people in remote areas, and I taught health classes at the local elementary school about exercise and hand hygiene. Also, while I was there, my community experienced a huge dengue fever outbreak, so I was able to help lead an education program about dengue prevention and mosquito control.

DENGUE FEVER = A VERY SERIOUS VIRUS TRANSMITTED BY MOSQUITOES IN THE TROPICS AND SUBTROPICS.

Did you get any additional training before you went to Cambodia?

For me, the most important part of my training was learning the Khmer language and learning about the Cambodian culture. It was crucial that I be able to communicate with my community in their own language. If I hadn't been able to speak Khmer, or hadn't understood the Cambodian culture, I wouldn't have been a successful volunteer.

What was your favorite part about volunteering with the Peace Corps?

My favorite part was getting to connect with people who are from such a different and distant part of the world from where I grew up. It was amazing to see that despite coming from very different cultures, we were able to communicate, understand each other, and love one another.

What did you learn from your service in the Peace Corps?

My service has taught me that there truly is hope in the world. I learned that people want to learn, they want to grow, and they want the best for all people. Despite the difficulties of life in rural Cambodia, people find ways to help one another, be happy, and celebrate together.

What are some of the necessary skills or traits for a Peace Corps volunteer?

In order to be a Peace Corps volunteer, you need to be brave, curious, patient, and kind. It seems like a lot to ask, but it really is a very tough job. You need to be brave enough to live very far away from your home, in a community that is probably very different from the one where you grew up. You need to be curious about other cultures and the way people live. You need to be patient with yourself and with the community members where you serve, as you'll be crossing very big gaps in culture and language. And you need to be kind to all the people you encounter as a Peace Corps volunteer. It's through kindness that you'll be able to see the true beauty of the Peace Corps. When you're kind to your community, they will reward you with an abundance of kindness in return.

75 WiLD & WACky!

Snail PATROL

You might not think of snails as being super threatening. Slow? Yes. Slimy? Sure. But threatening? Not so much. Well, it turns out that some species of snails are a serious threat.

In fact, giant African land snails (GALS), which are an invasive species (meaning they don't naturally occur in a country), cause such significant problems that it is illegal to own one in the United States.

Why are they such a problem? Because they're a huge hazard to agriculture—they eat more than 500 different kinds of crops! Even more amazing, they like to eat stucco and cement from the sides of houses, and it's possible they could make people very sick. The snails can carry the rat lungworm parasite, which can cause meningitis in humans and pets.

Several years ago, there was a large outbreak of these snails in South Florida. So, what now? These menacing mollusks had to go.

A GIANT AFRICAN LAND SNAIL (GALS)

ENTER THE SNAIL PATROL! Well, actually, they're members of the Florida Department of Agriculture and Consumer Services, but they do patrol for snails. In fact, they've already caught more than 150,000 GALS since 2011. Floridians are told to report any GALS sightings right away and to not touch the snails. Someone who has been trained to handle them and who is wearing the proper protective gear will come to remove them.

FIVE FASCINATING FACTS ABOUT GIANT AFRICAN LAND SNAILS

1 The first GALS were brought to the continental United States in 1966, when a boy brought them home to Miami from Hawaii to keep as pets. His grandmother put them out in her garden, and in just seven years, there were nearly 18,000 GALS in Florida. It took 10 years and more than one million dollars to squelch that particular infestation.

2 GALS can grow to be eight inches (20 cm) long, four inches (10 cm) wide, and weigh up to one pound (0.45 kg).

3 The Florida Department of Agriculture has successfully trained snail-sniffing dogs to locate these pesky mollusks.

4 In 2014, officials at Los Angeles International Airport intercepted a shipment of 67 live GALS from Nigeria.

5 Each GALS can lay up to 1,200 eggs a year and live up to 10 years.

Psychologist

Just like you might visit a doctor if something were bothering you physically, you can visit a psychologist if something is bothering you emotionally.

Psychologists are individuals with an advanced degree in psychology who diagnose mental, emotional, and behavioral health issues and treat patients with **talk therapy.** They don't prescribe medication (only a psychiatrist can do that), but they can work with patients to come up with helpful strategies for dealing with anxiety, stress, or depression. They also can help sort through big, **complicated feelings** during **difficult times,** such as a serious illness, the death of someone close, or ending a relationship.

77

PROFESSIONAL
O·R·G·A·N·I·Z·E·R

Whether it be your homework calendar,
your closet, or your life, these professionals
MAKE SENSE OF THE MAYHEM. They'll help
you to get organized and stay organized.

CAN YOU IMAGINE A WORLD WITHOUT LIGHT-BULBS, TOILET PAPER, WINDSHIELD WIPERS, OR PLAY-DOH?

Neither could the smart cookies who invented them.

They saw an opportunity to create something new that could help people and make them happy. Inventors think outside the box to come up with new ideas, solutions, and products to make life a little bit easier or just a little bit more fun.

INVENTOR

78

79

MEDITATION INSTRUCTOR

Practicing meditation helps strengthen attention and focus and quiet the mind. Meditation instructors teach people how to meditate and sometimes lead them in guided meditation.

YOU CAN HIRE SOMEONE TO WAIT IN A LONG LINE FOR YOU SO THAT YOU DON'T HAVE TO.

Instead of waiting hours for the store that's selling the cool new tech gadget to open, just hire a line waiter, or line sitter, to get there early and secure a spot for you at the front of the line. Then, you can sleep in and show up just as the store's opening its doors.

MEET ROBERT SAMUEL.

HE'S THE FOUNDER OF SAME OLE LINE DUDES (SOLD) IN NEW YORK CITY, U.S.A.

Here he sheds some light on what it's really like to wait in line for a living.

>>>

How much do you charge?

$25 for the first hour of waiting, and $10 for each additional half hour.

What are some of the most popular items that you wait in line for?

Cronuts—a croissant-doughnut pastry, Broadway theater tickets, iPhones, sneakers, parades, autographs, concerts, and free giveaways.

What's the longest you've waited in line? What was it for?

I waited in line for 48 hours, for the iPhone 6S.

What supplies do you bring with you when you wait?

I bring iPhones, a portable charger, my iPad, hand warmers, and lots of apps.

What's your favorite way to pass the time?

Netflix, Hulu, and Pandora!

What are your dos and don'ts for waiting in long lines?

Don't skip people and don't curse. Do count the people in front of you frequently, to make sure your place in the line stays the same. And always be friendly. If you're standing in line, you might as well make a friend.

81

REAL ESTATE AGENT

Looking to buy a new house? Looking to sell one? A real estate agent helps people buy or sell houses and other buildings or property.

WELCOME HOME!

FINANCIAL
PLANNER

82

Sometimes it can be hard to save money—especially when spending it is so fun. But, if you ever want to have enough for a big purchase—like a car, house, or awesome vacation—saving's the name of the game. Financial planners help their clients set long-term goals and make wise money moves.

inspiration station

What does success look like to you? Will you feel successful if the work you do is helping people? Do you want you or your work to be well known? Is making a certain amount of money important to you? Will you feel successful if you're able to balance a job with hobbies and a full life outside of work? Different people have different ideas of success. Make a list of five words or phrases that describe what it means to you to be "successful."

CHEF

83

Picture a **chef** in your mind. Fold in **some** fun.

Stir in a heaping handful of HAPPY.

Add a splash of **siLLy** and a *dash* of *delicious.* Then, whisk in some **whimsy.**

THERE. NOW YOU HAVE

LAURA MILLER,

VEGAN CHEF EXTRAORDINAIRE.

"I fell in love with produce when I was a kid, **running through the little orchard of fruit trees that my parents had,"** says Miller. She's since gone on to **turn that passion for produce** into a show on the digital video network Tastemade called *Raw. Vegan. Not Gross,* as well as a **cookbook** by the same name. So cool!

VEGAN =
A PERSON WHO DOESN'T EAT MEAT OR ANIMAL PRODUCTS, SUCH AS MEAT, EGGS, AND MILK.

WHEN DID YOU BECOME INTERESTED IN VEGAN COOKING?

I began eating and cooking vegan when I was about 18. I mostly taught myself—I just followed what interested me and did a lot of experimenting. Sometimes it was awesome, and sometimes it wasn't so great. But you can't get better at something unless you're willing to make some mistakes along the way! When I started making food for my friends to test out recipes, I realized I loved doing that, which motivated me to learn more and share more with those around me.

WHAT DID YOU DO TO IMPROVE YOUR COOKING SKILLS?

One thing I did was I got a job as a line cook and baker at a fancy restaurant, which was a crash course in the world of cooking professionally. I put my head down and worked, pedal to the metal, learning everything I could. Working in a kitchen is unlike any other job—you don't get paid a lot, you work your buns off, and you deal with a lot of stress ... but, man, it's fun! It made me stronger and a better worker, and made me fall in love with food even more. It also gave me the courage and knowledge to eventually start my own raw, vegan baking business, and later, launch my video series, *Raw. Vegan. Not Gross.*

HOW DID YOU COME UP WITH THAT NAME?

For a while when I was living in San Francisco, I ran my own business called Sidesaddle Kitchen. I sold raw, vegan desserts, something that can be a little "out there" for folks who have never really tried that kind of food before. So I put a big sign over my booth to make it extra clear. It said: "RAW. VEGAN. NOT GROSS."

I want everyone to know that raw food can taste incredible and make you feel great; it's not boring, bland rabbit food! My title and my recipes reflect that, and I'm proud and excited to share them with the world.

WHAT IS IT ABOUT COOKING THAT EXCITES YOU AND BRINGS YOU THE MOST JOY?

As a chef, I love the fun and energy food brings to my life. There's an electric feeling that comes from making and sharing food. That feeling is even more heightened when I can share how to make the food, and I get to see people empowered to create new things themselves.

WHAT ARE SOME OF THE NECESSARY SKILLS OR TRAITS OF SOMEONE WHO WOULD LIKE TO BE A CHEF?

To be a chef, you have to call on so many different traits. You have to be hardworking, resilient, and motivated. You have to be imaginative and generous with your time, energy, and creativity. You have to be cooperative, flexible, and patient—with others and yourself. You have to be humble enough to know you will always be learning, no matter how long you've been working at it. You have to be a little crazy and a lot fearless and be willing to make some real stinkers in order to figure out how to make winners.

YOU MAKE AMAZING FRUIT AND VEGETABLE WIGS AND JEWELRY—HOW DID THAT START?

I started taking funny photos with produce partly because I knew I needed to show who I was on my business's social media, but I was uncomfortable just putting shots of myself up there. Putting produce on, whether it was a chive wig or a lemon necklace, made it feel like an art project, so it was less intimidating. I want people to have fun with their food! It's something that nourishes and fuels our bods, but it also can be something really creative and joyful. My fruit jewelry and vegetable wigs are a really visual expression of that. They are a way for me to think outside the box and express myself with food beyond cooking with it.

84

CEO of the National Geographic Society, Gary Knell. Gary oversees the nonprofit side of the Society.

DIRECTOR OF A NONPROFIT

A nonprofit is a charitable organization that benefits the public, not just the people working for it. Any extra money that's made by the organization goes to its MISSION, rather than to the employees. There are many nonprofits that work to improve society and help people, as well as protect animals and the environment.

211

SKY *Writer*

YOU'VE HEARD OF A MESSAGE IN A BOTTLE, BUT WHAT ABOUT A MESSAGE IN THE CLOUDS?

Skywriters are HIGHLY SKILLED PILOTS who fly up, down, and all around while their planes emit white smoke made from a special paraffin oil to SPELL OUT MESSAGES in the sky. The letters, which can be up to a mile (1.6 km) high and a mile (1.6 km) wide each, are most easily read on clear, calm days, since wind does to skywriting what shaking does to an Etch-A-Sketch image.

85

WiLd &
wAcKy!

86 HIST

ORIAN

THESE HISTORY BUFFS LOVE LEARNING ABOUT THE PAST—what happened, why it happened, and who was involved. Often historians specialize and become experts on a particular topic. They then share their extensive knowledge with others as teachers, professors, museum employees, tour guides, and authors.

For almost every holiday,

major life event, and even emotion, *there's a card for that.* Some cards rhyme, *some sing,* **some are SiLLy, and some are serious.** But, all cards begin as a **KERNEL OF INSPIRATION** in someone's **BRAIN.**

FUN FACT!

Americans buy about **6.5 BILLION GREETING CARDS** each year! That's a lot of **BIRTHDAYS, BAT MITZVAHS,** and **"BE MINE"S!**

TO BE A GREETING CARD WRITER, you need to be **creative,** have a **great vocabulary,** and be able to **express complex feelings** clearly. When people see what you've written, you want them to think, **Aha! That's exactly how I feel!**

TEACHER

Great teachers can have a **BIG IMPACT.** A really great teacher can make an otherwise **DULL** subject **FASCINATING,** encourage students to **DREAM BIG,** and motivate a class to **WORK HARD.**

Think about your **FAVORITE** teachers. What are the qualities that make them **EXCEPTIONAL?** If you were a teacher, what would you do the same as your teachers and what would you do differently?

89 COMPUTER PROGRAMMER

To communicate with a computer, you just have to know the right code. And it's not even a secret code. **ANYONE CAN LEARN IT!**

Humans and computers don't speak the same language. Computers use a language called code, which is a mix of letters, symbols, and numbers. So if we humans want a computer to perform a specific task, the instructions need to be translated into code. The person who does this is a computer programmer.

FUN FACT!

When the White House decorates for the holidays, each U.S. state and territory gets to trim its own tree in President's Park near the White House. In 2014, though, the tree trimmings went high-tech. Thanks to the National Park Service and Google's Made with Code, girls from across the country could **CONTROL THE COLORS AND PATTERNS OF THE LIGHTS BY WRITING DIGITAL CODE,** all from their personal computers.

Balloon twister

90

WiLd & wAcKy!

WHAT ONCE WAS A COOL PARTY TRICK IS NOW A BOOMING BUSINESS.

Balloon twisters work at restaurants, company picnics, birthday parties, and more. And with a few balloons and a flick of the wrist, they can twist up some pretty wild creations. They can make helicopters and hats, dinosaurs and fire-breathing dragons. Professional balloon twister Todd Neufeld even made a balloon replica of President Obama at a Fourth of July party at the White House. It took a whopping 25 balloons!

91

PERSONAL
Trainer

From sit-ups to squats, pull-ups to planks, personal trainers help their clients set and achieve fitness goals. Just one more! **YOU CAN DO IT!**

92

confectioner

FRUIT CHEWS AND **CHOCOLATE,**
CARAMELS AND CANDY CANES.

A **confectioner** is someone who makes
and sells delicious **candies** and **sweets.**
Now that's one **sweet dream job.**

Good things come to those who work hard to achieve them. Be prepared to put in the time and effort to reach your goals.

. . . .

"Genius is one percent inspiration and ninety-nine percent perspiration."

—Thomas Edison

I'M A CHOCOLATE MOUSE, NOT CHOCOLATE MOUSSE.

THINK OF A ROLLER COASTER.

Every sweat-inducing second of a climb to the top and every stomach-flopping drop. Every cheek-flapping loop-de-loop and every spine-tingling turn. Someone gets to dream all of that up. And that someone is a roller coaster designer.

MEET KOREY T. KIEPERT, roller coaster engineer and partner at the Gravity Group.

93

ROLLER COASTER DESIGNER

CÚ CHULAINN COASTER
Tayto Park, Ireland

Q HOW DID YOU BECOME INTERESTED IN BECOMING A ROLLER COASTER DESIGNER?

A I grew up in a suburb of Detroit [in Michigan, U.S.A]. When I was young, my parents would take my brother and me to an amusement park called Cedar Point. Those trips really inspired us. We even set up a small amusement park in my brother's closet, using cereal boxes and trinkets that we found.

My first roller coaster ride was on the Cedar Creek Mine Ride, which was a small steel coaster, when I was about 11. On one trip to Cedar Point, my brother and I rode every single one of the roller coasters. Then, at some point, I stumbled upon an article in *Smithsonian* magazine about roller coaster designers. This lightbulb went off: Someone had to do that job, and someday, that someone could be me!

So, I wrote letters to some of the roller coaster companies asking them about working for them someday. Some companies wrote back and were encouraging, and others were not. I still have a letter from a prominent roller coaster designer who told me that the odds of me designing roller coasters were so small that I should give up the dream and do something else.

I'm glad I didn't listen to him.

Q WHAT DID YOU STUDY IN SCHOOL TO BE A ROLLER COASTER DESIGNER?

A Math and science were a big part of my education. When I was in college, I tried to choose classes that would be useful to designing roller coasters. I was studying to be a mechanical engineer, but I got special permission to take some extra structural engineering classes that were offered by the civil engineering department, like steel design and timber design.

TIMBER!
Walibi Rhone Alpes, France

Q WHAT ARE SOME OF THE WAYS YOU DREAM UP NEW ROLLER COASTER IDEAS?

A It varies from project to project. Sometimes, we are given a big blank space and told to fill it however we'd like. Other times, there are features—like terrain, buildings, or even other rides—that determine where a ride can go or what it can do. But, honestly, sometimes the more restrictive the site, the more creative we are with our rides. For example, there was a ride that we designed for a park in Sweden on a very compact site. We ended up having to build our ride to go over and under other roller coasters, and half of it was elevated on a building! But in the end, it was a very unique and exciting ride.

Q WHAT IS YOUR FAVORITE PART OF THE DESIGN PROCESS?

A I like visiting a park that is considering a ride and walking around the site with the park owner, capturing their vision for it. It's my goal, always, to exceed their expectations. Then, I like being there for that first ride, when the owner experiences what we created. Those are the most electrifying times for me.

Q WHICH ONE OF THE ROLLER COASTERS THAT YOU'VE DESIGNED IS YOUR FAVORITE TO RIDE?

A The Cú Chulainn Coaster near Dublin, Ireland, is one of my favorites. It's packed with airtime—that weightless feeling you get cresting a hill—and has some nice features, like tunnels, high banking, and incredible drops.

My family joined me in Ireland during the commissioning of the ride, and it was great bringing my kids to the jobsite to show them firsthand what I had been working on. Three of the four were even tall enough to enjoy some rides on it!

231

94

EMERGENCY MEDICAL TECHNICIAN

Emergency medical technicians (EMTs) need to be quick and calm under pressure. They're often first on the scene and are trained to give lifesaving medical treatment. They respond to accidents and 9-1-1 calls and can give CPR, treat a wound, and quickly get the sick and injured to a hospital.

FOLEY

95

WiLd & wAcKy!

ARTIST

Doors creaking. Plates shattering. A fire roaring. Footsteps crunching on a pile of leaves. Many of these everyday sound effects in TV shows and movies are added by a Foley artist after the footage is filmed. Sometimes, the action is recreated in a sound booth to get just the right noise. But more often, the sound is constructed using objects you wouldn't expect.

HERE ARE A FEW SOUND EFFECTS AND WHAT A FOLEY ARTIST MIGHT USE TO ACHIEVE THEM.

- **SNOW CRUNCHING** = SQUISHING CORN STARCH IN A LEATHER POUCH
- **HORSE HOOVES** = CLANKING THE HALVES OF A COCONUT SHELL ON THE GROUND
- **RAIN** = SPRINKLING DRY RICE OR SAND ONTO A METAL COOKIE SHEET
- **FIRE** = CRINKLING A SHEET OF CELLOPHANE
- **WINGS FLAPPING** = FLAPPING A PAIR OF LEATHER GLOVES

SUPREME COURT justice

96

The Supreme Court is the BIG CHEESE, or the HEAD HONCHO, of ALL OF THE COURTS IN THE UNITED STATES. The justices are the individuals who listen to cases and make the decisions. There are NINE SUPREME COURT JUSTICES in the United States.

All justices must have been trained in the law, and to become one, an individual must be NOMINATED BY THE PRESIDENT. Then the Senate will VOTE on whether or not to confirm the president's nomination. Once on the Supreme Court, a justice can stay there FOR LIFE, unless he or she chooses to resign or is impeached.

Most of the cases heard by the Supreme Court are ones that have already been ruled on by lower courts in the country. But the people involved in these cases think that the rulings weren't fair or just, so they ask the Supreme Court to review them. It's the justices' job to make sure that the lower court's decision ABIDES BY THE U.S. CONSTITUTION, which is the supreme law of the country.

FUN FACT!

The U.S. CONSTITUTION has 4,543 WORDS (including the signatures). It is the OLDEST and SHORTEST WRITTEN CONSTITUTION of any major government in the world.

SPECIALIST

Animals need special accommodations to MAKE SURE THEY THRIVE when they're in a zoo, away from their natural habitat. They need to EAT SIMILAR FOODS as they would IN THE WILD, do similar activities—like climbing, swinging, or digging—and even face similar challenges that keep their BODIES AND MINDS IN TIP-TOP SHAPE.

To give animals a more AUTHENTIC EXPERIENCE, animal enrichment specialists will do things like hide the animals' food so that they have to work to find it. They'll PLAY SOUNDS OF NATURE and other wild animal calls, and they'll even SPRAY THE SMELLS of the animals' natural predators and prey. When it comes to making zoo animals FEEL MORE AT HOME, these specialized zoologists leave no stone (or chew toy) unturned.

239

What if your job was to play? And what if you didn't have to put away your toys and get to work . . .

because toys were your work?

241

That'd be pretty awesome, right?

MEET JOHN WARDEN. He designs Transformers toys for Hasbro. He's known since he was a kid that he never wanted to outgrow his toys. In fact, when he was in the fifth grade, he was given the assignment to write to a company that does work he might be interested in doing as an adult. So, he wrote to a toy company. And to his surprise, the president of the company actually wrote him back and invited him to the design studio.

> "I was given a great behind-the-scenes tour of the facility and got to meet with some of the designers and engineers of the toys I loved," says Warden. "After seeing the process firsthand, and how creative and fun it was, I decided that toy design was what I wanted to do when I grew up."

And he does. Here Warden shares what it's like to work hard by playing hard.

WHAT ARE SOME OF THE WAYS YOU DREAM UP NEW TOY IDEAS?
Cool new ideas can come from anywhere. But one of my favorite places to look for new toy ideas is in nature. By looking closely at trees, plants, animals, and geology, I begin to see movements and actions that could become a new toy feature or play pattern.

As a dad, I get inspired when I play with my own kids. There are few things in this world more powerful than a kid's imagination. Some of my favorite projects I've worked on have come from ideas my kids and I have stumbled upon when we play together.

WHAT'S YOUR FAVORITE PART OF DESIGNING TOYS?
It is a powerful feeling to let your imagination take you to new places and to create new worlds, new heroes, and new villains. Through sketches and models, I can bring my dreams to life and share them with people.

WHAT ARE SOME OF THE TOYS YOU'VE WORKED ON? IS THERE ONE THAT YOU PARTICULARLY ENJOYED CREATING, OR ONE YOU'RE MOST PROUD OF?
I've worked on Star Wars toys, Pokémon toys, G.I. Joe toys, and now Transformers toys. My favorite toy I've worked on recently was Devastator for the Transformers Generations Combiner Wars toy line. Devastator was a giant lime green and purple robot that was made up of six different evil Decepticons known as

the Constructicons. Each of these robots changed into a construction vehicle, like a power shovel or a bulldozer.

As a kid, I had a much smaller version of Devastator that my little brother and I played with together. It was a great experience to bring him to life for a new generation of kids to enjoy.

WHAT'S YOUR ADVICE FOR SOMEONE WHO WANTS TO DESIGN TOYS?

Draw all the time. If your drawing doesn't turn out the way you want it to, or if something is wrong – keep going. Also (and this one is important!) really look at how things are made. Learning how things work and how we as humans interact with them is a critical part of understanding what makes a good product.

WHAT'S THE SECRET TO FINDING YOUR DREAM JOB?

Never give up. In elementary school, I told myself that I wanted to grow up and design action figures and Transformers for a living. Now, as an adult, I have the job I always wanted. Along the way, you will have plenty of obstacles in your path, and life will try to throw you curveballs. There will be people who tell you that it's too hard or it's not possible. Don't believe them.

If you believe in your dreams and are determined to never give up, anything is possible. Your imagination is the most powerful thing in the world.

JOHN WARDEN IN ELEMENTARY SCHOOL

WARDEN EXPLAINS HOW TOYS GO FROM AN IDEA IN SOMEONE'S HEAD TO THE NEW "IT" GADGET ON THE STORE SHELF.

1 The design process starts with brainstorming and drawing rough ideas, called thumbnail sketches, on paper.

2 Then, after conversations with fellow designers and engineers and lots of research, those initial ideas evolve into refined concept art, which can either be 2-D illustrations or 3-D sketch models.

3 Next, all of the concept art is looked at together, and decisions are made as to which designs make sense to take to the next level.

4 Then a "design control" drawing is created, which is essentially a rough blueprint for creating a test model, known as a prototype. This prototype is used for several types of tests in which people interact with the design—for example, picking it up, seeing if it feels right in their hands, or if it does the job that it was intended to do.

5 Once the prototype is finalized, the designer works with an engineer to bring the product to life through mass-production.

Novelist

Never, never give up!

When J.K. Rowling finished writing her first book, *Harry Potter and the Sorcerer's Stone*, 12 publishing houses turned it down before it was finally accepted. Can you imagine if she'd thrown in the towel after the 11th rejection? Thankfully, she didn't, and since then, she's written six more Harry Potter books, and there have been eight movies made based on the series. There are Harry Potter theme parks, Harry Potter video games, and even a stage play in London, *Harry Potter and the Cursed Child*.

Any world you can imagine, any character you can conjure, you can write about. A novelist's head is filled with **fictional people** and the lives they lead. These lives can **fill the pages of a book** and then **become real** in the **mind of a reader.**

100 WiLd & wAcky!

Chief Happiness Officer

YEP!

This smile-inducing job title is really a thing. Research has continued to find that HAPPY employees make BETTER employees. Happy people are more productive, they're more likely to stay with a company, they're greater problem-solvers, and they get along better with their co-workers. So, companies are making it a priority to make their workers happier. One way they're accomplishing that? By designating a chief happiness officer to up the joy quotient.

CAREER LIST

Here's a list of the 100 jobs featured in this book. This list is by no means comprehensive. There are so many jobs, careers, and life paths out there that we will have to save for a follow-up book! And life is long and holds many surprises, so don't be afraid to aim for more than one! Delve into your creative side, think outside the box, and don't listen to people who say you can't accomplish anything you set your mind to. Not even the sky's the limit. Just ask Shannon Walker (p. 84)!

1. Ice-Cream Flavor Developer
2. Mushroom Forager
3. Beekeeper
4. Lyricist
5. Golf Ball Diver
6. TV Writer
7. Natural History Photographer
8. Voice-over Actor
9. App Developer
10. Professional Pusher
11. Sports Team Physician
12. Hollywood Animal Trainer
13. Fight Choreographer
14. Music Photographer
15. Snake Milker
16. Radio Host
17. National Park Service Employee
18. Adventure Guide
19. Party Planner
20. Professional Bridesmaid
21. Animal Groomer
22. Recipe Tester
23. Movie Trailer Editor
24. Primatologist
25. Iceberg Tracker
26. Astronomer
27. Paleontologist
28. Art Conservationist
29. Mathematician
30. Make-Up Artist
31. Political Speechwriter
32. Astronaut
33. Rodeo Clown
34. Perfumer
35. Pet Food Taster
36. Farrier
37. Woodworker
38. Fashion Designer

INDEX

Boldface indicates illustrations. If illustrations are included within a page span, the entire span is boldface.

Find Out More

Grab a parent and visit these websites for more information!

1. nationalgeographic.com/
explorers
2. nasa.gov/audience/forstudents
3. nps.gov/kids
4. events.nationalgeographic.com
5. si.edu

For my grandmothers, Emily Burrell and Beverly Gerry,
two of the smartest, strongest, bravest women I know.
I'd love to be like you when I grow up. I love you.
—LG

Since 1888, the National Geographic Society has funded more than 12,000 research, exploration, and preservation projects around the world. The Society receives funds from National Geographic Partners LLC, funded in part by your purchase. A portion of the proceeds from this book supports this vital work.

NATIONAL GEOGRAPHIC and Yellow Border Design are trademarks of the National Geographic Society, used under license.

For more information, please visit nationalgeographic.com, call 1-877-873-6846, or write to the following address:

National Geographic Partners, LLC
1145 17th Street N.W.
Washington, D.C. 20036-4688 U.S.A.

Visit us online at nationalgeographic.com/books

For librarians and teachers: ngchildrensbooks.org

More for kids from National Geographic: natgeokids.com

For rights or permissions inquiries, please contact National Geographic Books Subsidiary Rights: bookrights@natgeo.com

The publisher would like to acknowledge Callie Broaddus, Julide Dengel, Anne LeongSon, Ashita Murgai, Sanjida Rashid, Gus Tello, Stephanie White, and Breanna Young for their creative input; photo editor Hillary Leo; and editor Ariane Szu-Tu.

Art Directed by Callie Broaddus and Sanjida Rashid.

Library of Congress Cataloging-in-Publication Data

Names: Gerry, Lisa, author.
Title: 100 things to be when you grow up / by Lisa M. Gerry.
Other titles: One hundred things to be when you grow up
Description: Washington, D.C. : National Geographic Kids, [2017] | Includes index.
Identifiers: LCCN 2016029013| ISBN 9781426327117 (pbk. : alk. paper) | ISBN 9781426327124 (library binding : alk. paper)
Subjects: LCSH: Vocational guidance--Juvenile literature. | Occupations--Juvenile literature.
Classification: LCC HF5381.2 .G47 2017 | DDC 331.702--dc23
LC record available at lccn.loc.gov/2016029013

Printed in China
21/PPS/4 (SC)
21/PPS/2 (RLB)